GCSE English Literature for AQA
Poetry Student Book

Trevor Millum and Andy Mort
Series editor: Peter Thomas

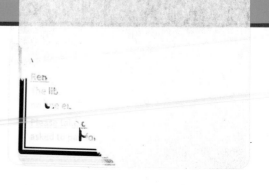

CAMBRIDGE
UNIVERSITY PRESS

University Printing House, Cambridge CB2 8BS, United Kingdom

Cambridge University Press is part of the University of Cambridge.

It furthers the University's mission by disseminating knowledge in the pursuit of education, learning and research at the highest international levels of excellence.

www.cambridge.org

Information on this title:
www.cambridge.org/9781107454712 (Paperback)
www.cambridge.org/9781107454729 (Cambridge Elevate-enhanced Edition)
www.cambridge.org/9781107454682 (Paperback + Cambridge Elevate-enhanced Edition)

© Cambridge University Press 2015

First published 2015

Printed in Dubai by Oriental Press

A catalogue record for this publication is available from the British Library

ISBN 978-1-107-45471-2 Paperback
ISBN 978-1-107-45472-9 Cambridge Elevate-enhanced Edition
ISBN 978-1-107-45468-2 Paperback + Cambridge Elevate-enhanced Edition

Additional resources for this publication at www.cambridge.org/ukschools

Contents

Exploring and comparing poetry

INTRODUCTION

Welcome to your AQA GCSE English Literature poetry book, with poems from leading poets from 1789 up until the present day. We hope you will enjoy these poems during your GCSE course and later in life.

Many of the poems deal with things that you are already familiar with – growing up, family ties and relationships. They also deal with power and conflict beyond the personal. There are poems that will reflect your own ideas and others that may challenge or even change the way you think.

Your student book will help you make the most of the poems and of your GCSE. It will develop your appreciation of poetry and of the methods poets use to share their insights and engage the reader. It will also develop your skills in writing about and comparing poems for GCSE English Literature.

Here's how we have organised the book for you:

Exploring and comparing poetry shows you areas that are important in reading and responding to poetry at GCSE and outlines the thinking behind some of the approaches in this book. It also gives you an understanding of differences in poetry through time – and how is it relevant to you today.

Poems past and present – the AQA Anthology helps you to understand, explore and compare poems in your chosen cluster of either 'Love and relationships' or 'Power and conflict'. Your learning in this section also prepares you for exploring and comparing unseen poems.

Unseen poetry develops your skills in responding to poems you have not met before. You will draw on and adapt what you have learned in studying Cluster 1 or Cluster 2 to help you tackle the unseen poetry section of your exam.

Preparing for your exam gives you practice and guidance on each poetry question in the exam, with examples of answers, so you can use the skills you have developed and assess where your skills are strong and where to focus your effort to improve.

On Cambridge Elevate your learning will be extended to new dimensions. Here you will find:

- readings of the poems – some by the poets themselves
- textplorations – experiences in media that take you to the heart of the poem.

We hope that you will enjoy using these resources, not only to support your GCSE study, but to see that poetry has plenty to say about life around you – and within you.

The Cambridge University Press team

POETRY AND GCSE ENGLISH LITERATURE

Your GCSE course in poetry has been designed so that you experience a range of poetry from 1789 to the present day and develop skills in approaching 'unseen' poems.

In the AQA Anthology there are two clusters of 15 poems, with a choice of 'Love and relationships' or 'Power and conflict'. Your work with these poems will also develop your skills in responding to other poems that are new to you.

At the end of your GCSE course in English Literature you will sit an exam. The Literature exam has two papers:

- **Paper 1 Shakespeare and the 19th-century novel**, which is worth 40% of your GCSE
- **Paper 2 Modern texts and poetry**, which is worth 60% of your GCSE.

POETRY IN THE EXAM

Paper 2 Modern texts and poetry has three sections:

- **Section A Modern texts**, where you answer one essay question from a choice of two on your studied modern **prose** or drama text.
- **Section B Poetry**, where you answer one question on comparing poems from your chosen cluster of the anthology, 'Love and relationships' or 'Power and conflict'.
- **Section C Unseen poetry**, where you write about a poem that you have not seen before and then compare this poem with a second unseen poem.

GCSE ENGLISH LITERATURE ASSESSMENT OBJECTIVES

The Assessment Objectives (AOs) form the basis for the GCSE mark scheme. For poetry, the assessment is against AO1, AO2 and AO3 for Section B, and AO1 and AO2 for Section C:

Assessment Objective 1

Read and respond to texts. Students should be able to:

- maintain a critical style and develop an informed personal response
- use textual references, including quotations, to support and illustrate interpretations.

Assessment Objective 2

Analyse the language, **form** and **structure** used by a writer to create meanings and effects, using relevant subject terminology where appropriate.

Assessment Objective 3

Show understanding of the relationships between texts and the **contexts** in which they were written.

LITERATURE SKILLS AND STUDY FOCUS AREAS

Most of the skills you develop in your study of poetry will be the same as those in other parts of your GCSE English reading. You will develop your core skills to show **understanding**, **interpretation** and **analysis**. We will explore these skills, along with the following study focus areas, in this book.

Ideas, attitudes and feelings

These amount to **content** – what's in the poems. The important thing to remember is that they are three different things.

- **Ideas** are the thoughts that explain or result from an experience.
- **Attitudes** are the positions or postures we adopt when facing experiences.

- **Feelings** are the emotions people feel, which are often quite different from their attitudes and ideas.

For example, with the poem 'Follower' by Seamus Heaney (Cluster 1 Unit 10), you could say that:

- The **idea** is that it takes skill to be an expert in horse-ploughing.
- The **attitude** is admiration for his father's skill.
- The **feeling** is sadness that his father is no longer the same as when he was younger.

Language, form and structure

These amount to the way the poems are written – the **writer's methods**. Again, the important thing to remember is that they are three different things.

For example, with the poem 'Follower', you could say that:

- The **language** is drawn from knowledge of life on the farm.
- The **form** is six four-line **verses** with an ABAB **rhyme scheme** with some **half-rhymes**.
- The **structure** is three verses describing his father in the past, two verses describing the writer in the past and a final verse describing both of them as they are now, and their changing relationship over time.

Language includes, for example:

- visual **images** – such as connections made by **simile** and **metaphor**
- aural appeal – such as sound effects made by **assonance** and **alliteration**
- word choice and word order – selecting, for example, particular verbs for effect
- voice – for example of the poet or the **persona** in the poem, using a particular idiom or style
- address – for example the **tone** of the poem/poet/persona – personal, argumentative, reflective or challenging.

Form and **structure** include, for example:

- **sonnets** – 14 lines, usually divided into two groups of eight and six, with a fixed rhyme scheme
- **dramatic monologues** – presenting events from the point of view of a character, not the writer
- **free verse** – no rhyme scheme but may have a regular number of syllables
- **rhyme** – may be full rhyme or half-rhyme
- **rhythm** – may be regular, irregular or mixed.

 All words in orange are explained in the glossary section at the end of the book.

with a single pluck
Of reins, the sweating team turned round
And back into the land.

(From 'Follower' by Seamus Heaney, Cluster 1 Unit 10)

DEVELOPING WRITTEN RESPONSE SKILLS

Put simply, the levels of GCSE might broadly be put into three categories of **understanding**, **explaining** and **conceptualising**.

This book helps you to identify the level you are working at, and what skills you need to improve. It supports you in writing that is focused on the GCSE study areas.

From comment to conceptualising

A feature of the anthology units is to help you develop your responses to poems, moving from the ability to comment on 'facts' about the poem to using your understanding and interpretation skills to explain feelings, motives or reasons, and presenting ideas that develop and extend meaning. For example look at the following responses to the extract from the poem 'The Prelude' by William Wordsworth (Cluster 2 Unit 3):

Simple comment: It is about stealing a boat.

Explained response: It is about stealing a boat and feeling excited then guilty about it.

Developed response: It is about a Romantic poet's belief that nature can affect human morality just like religion or laws can.

Writing with focus

A further feature of the anthology units is to develop **focused writing**. When you respond to a question on poems you need to show that your response is dealing with essential GCSE skills, and linked to specific details of the text, whether you are comparing poems or responding to a single poem. You will need to do this in a focused way when writing under timed conditions in the exam, making your points quickly and linking your chosen textual detail to a clear purpose.

The following examples can help you develop these writing skills. Every sentence has to count!

Writer's purpose

I think he wants the reader to feel …

She probably did this to make the reader think …

The writer wants to show that …

The ending/beginning is intended to surprise the reader …

The writer was writing to change/challenge the view that …

The writer was writing to entertain/warn/celebrate … , so chose to …

And growing still in stature the grim shape
Towered up between me and the stars

(From 'The Prelude' by William Wordsworth, Cluster 2 Unit 3)

Feelings

You can see the writer's feelings in the statement …

The person in the poem's feelings are obvious when …

This gives me the feeling that …

Words like … and … are usually used to express feelings of …

The feeling of … in the poem changes when …

The feeling of … increases as the poem goes on, as you can see by …

Ideas and perspectives

He explains this by saying it is like …

This creates the idea that she may have …

This is a gloomy/optimistic attitude because …

She writes this because she thinks that …

You could say this is a man's way of looking at …

This **perspective** makes you realise that …

Language

The words that create this mood are …

All the verbs she uses suggest violence/admiration, such as …

There is a pattern in her use of adjectives and adverbs, which nearly all …

The phrase … puts together very different words in order to …

The language in the poem changes from … to …

He could have used the word … here, but chose to use the word … because …

Literary techniques

He chooses the word … here to express his fear, but also to rhyme with …

The short/long vowels in this line make it seem more …

He uses similes that all relate to the activity of …

She repeats the 's' sound so that the line sounds as if it is hissed, to show …

The sentence is carried over to the next line so that the verb 'slumped' is given more …

He carries this metaphor on by …

Structure and form

The poem can be divided into two/three/… stages of …

The poem starts with a description of an event that involves … , then the poet's feeling about … , then ends with the idea that …

The first eight lines are about … , then the last six lines are about what the writer thinks about …

It is a dramatic monologue, so the voice in the poem is not the author's, which makes it …

The poem moves from statements based on 'I' to those based on 'You' to those based on 'We', which …

The story is **chronological**, but the last verse …

Interpretation and relevance to me or others

I think the writer wrote this poem because she wanted to …

The word … has several meanings but the one I think fits best here is …

This reason he did this/thought this was because he …

I don't agree with this, but a lot of people would say …

There are two ways of looking at this, such as …

Contexts

This may have been what a lot of people thought at the time, but today …

I think I wouldn't do that, but if I was in that situation, maybe I would because …

This may seem unusual, but the writer is exploring how a person from that context would behave when …

What strikes you when you read this poem after … is how different …

The poem reflects some of the social conditions and ideas about society that …

You could say that what he writes about here is/is not relevant to today because …

COMPARING POEMS

In your exam you will need to write a comparison for Section B (anthology poems) and Section C (unseen poems). This guidance will help you develop skills to write a focused response when comparing poems in the anthology.

 For more guidance on writing a focused response in Section C of your exam, go to the Unseen poetry section.

Poems to compare

You will find ideas for poems to compare in each unit of the anthology clusters. Unit 16, at the end of each cluster, will help you develop these skills further, using four poem pairings as examples. The pairings are listed here.

There are many ways of comparing different poems. These are examples to which you can add your own ideas. Your choice of a poem to compare in the exam will depend on the 'named' poem and the focus of the question.

Cluster 1: Love and relationships

The suggested comparisons are:

- Pair 1 'Walking Away' and 'Follower'
- Pair 2 'Neutral Tones' and 'Winter Swans'
- Pair 3 'Mother, any distance' and 'Before You Were Mine'
- Pair 4 'Love's Philosophy' and 'The Farmer's Bride'.

Areas of comparison might include similarities and differences in, for example:

- love relationships including passionate feelings, longing, broken relationships, healed relationships, tragic endings, public relationships, private relationships

- family relationships between parents, children, and grandparents, remembering, parents' perspectives, children's perspectives, relationships at different points in time, letting go, independence, dependence

- relationships between humans and nature, influenced by nature or expressed by using nature

- the voices/speakers of the poems, how the poets have expressed their ideas through the structure, form and language of the poems.

Cluster 2: Power and conflict

The suggested comparisons are:

- Pair 1 'Bayonet Charge' and 'Exposure'
- Pair 2 'Storm on the Island' and 'Ozymandias'
- Pair 3 'Kamikaze' and 'The Charge of the Light Brigade'
- Pair 4 'London' and the extract from 'The Prelude'.

Areas of comparison might include similarities and differences in, for example:

- power and conflict in private relationships, public relationships, families and across generations

- power and conflict in war; the effect of power and conflict on family relationships, professional contexts, military contexts

- power and conflict in nature; nature as hostile; physical power of nature; harmony with nature

- power and conflict in status, culture, identity, loyalties

- the voices/speakers of the poems, how the poets have expressed their ideas through the structure, form and language of the poems.

Writing your comparison

You may find the following words and phrases useful to make it clear that you are **comparing**, not just writing about the poems separately:

- to show **similarity**: similarly, likewise, equally, just as, both
- to show **difference**: whereas, on the other hand, in contrast, instead, however.

Use the following examples to guide and develop your comparison of poems.

Sample comments on **content**:

'Follower' and 'Walking Away' are <u>both</u> about father/son relationships, <u>but</u> in the first poem the poet is looking back on childhood as an adult, <u>whereas</u> in the second the father is looking back on memories of his grown-up son.

The **settings** of <u>both</u> 'Storm on the Island' and 'Ozymandias' are remote, the former being set on an island battered by powerful winds, and the latter being set in the desert where an exposed statue has been destroyed by nature, presumably sandstorms.

Sample comments on **language**:

Winter settings are important in <u>both</u> 'Neutral Tones' and 'Winter Swans'. Hardy describes a bare, depressing scene, using phrases like 'starving sod'. <u>However</u>, <u>although</u> the landscape is 'waterlogged' in Sheers's poem, nature is kinder, and the swans help to bring the couple closer, setting an example by 'tipping in unison'.

Owen and Hughes <u>both</u> use violent language to create a terrifying picture of First World War battlefields, for example 'shot-slashed furrows' in 'Bayonet Charge' and 'sudden successive flights of bullets streak the silence' in 'Exposure', <u>but</u> Owen also uses **contrasting** gentler language to describe the weather, for example 'sidelong flowing flakes'.

Sample comments on **structure**:

'Kamikaze' and 'The Charge of the Light Brigade' <u>both</u> describe war experiences and build their poems up towards key 'questions' about views of honour ('glory' and 'shame'), <u>but</u> Garland uses a time-shift before the last two verses to make a contrast, <u>whereas</u> Tennyson presents the action more continuously, using rhyme and repetition to create drama and **pace**.

Duffy and Armitage present their ideas and feelings about their mothers in different forms. Duffy describes how she imagines her mother's carefree behaviour before she was born in four verse 'paragraphs', ending the poem with the phrase 'before you were mine' to echo the poem's title. <u>However</u>, Armitage uses an **extended metaphor** to structure his ideas. The first part of the poem describes how the mother provides support, then it changes direction halfway through to focus on his move towards independence, creating a contrast.

That glamorous love lasts
where you sparkle and waltz and laugh
before you were mine.

(From 'Before You Were Mine')

POETRY THROUGH TIME

Poetry goes back before reading and print. Novels, needing a reader to deal with possibly hundreds of pages, did not emerge until the 18th century, but poetry was alive and well 4,000 years before. Sadly, because early poetry was not written down, most of it has not survived.

Poetry began as a public stand-up entertainment, with the poet reciting from memory stories about battles, love and adventures with strange creatures and monsters. Poetry was the TV and internet of its day – a mix to suit all audiences.

Well-off people, such as lords and kings, acted as patrons, hosting audiences and paying the poet. Many of the poems would be designed to flatter those who paid the fee, and appeal to their guests.

These oral poems were popular in various European cultures. In ancient Greece, Homer recited poems about the travels of the hero king Odysseus; in ancient Rome, Virgil recited similar poems about Aeneas. In Britain, the greatest oral poem was about the heroic deeds of Beowulf and his slaying of the monster Grendel.

Drama, with live actors, makes action visible on stage or elsewhere. Poetry had to appeal to the ear – with sound, and to the imagination – through visual images, to make the audiences imagine what they could not see. Poets dealt in the drama of the human voice. Poetry's advantage was that it was more convenient and cheaper, because it came to the audience, not the other way round.

Some poets keep the stand-up performance tradition going today. Poets such as John Agard (see Cluster 2 Unit 15) make their living as much by performing in public as publishing their work in books and magazines. Rap poems work best in live performance.

POETRY AND YOU

You may have had good experiences with poems, or perhaps you have read poems that didn't do anything for you. Whatever your experience, you will find that in this book there are poems that are about things that you already know about, already think about and already do.

Has your life so far involved relationships that you care about, people you love, feelings of courage, anger, frustration, or moments of laughter or surprise? If your answer is 'yes' to any of these questions, there are poems that will reflect your experiences and which are there to be enjoyed.

Poems past and present

This section is designed for everyone studying the AQA Anthology. It develops your skills in reading and comparing the poems in your chosen cluster. Each of the clusters contains 15 poems. The poems in each cluster are thematically linked and were written between 1789 and the present day.

THE POETRY CLUSTERS

You will be studying just one of the two clusters, although if you do read poems from the other cluster, that will be very good practice for the 'unseen poetry' part of your question paper. You should study all 15 poems in your chosen cluster and be prepared to compare any of them in the examination.

The anthology poems cover most of what matters in human life: love and relationships, and power and conflict. This book will help you understand the poems, appreciate the way they have been written and prepare you for successful answers in your Literature exam.

POEMS PAST AND PRESENT

Poetry comes in a variety of forms. Some are narrative, telling a story. Others are dramatic monologues – presenting a story or event from the point of view of a character – such as 'The Farmer's Bride' (Cluster 1 Unit 6) or 'My Last Duchess' (Cluster 2 Unit 4). Other poems set out to celebrate something, such as 'Letters from Yorkshire' (Cluster 1 Unit 8) or 'Tissue' (Cluster 2 Unit 12). Some are written in praise of a person, such as 'Follower' (Cluster 1 Unit 10) or 'War

Photographer' (Cluster 2 Unit 11), or to bring to life a minor or a major event from the past, such as 'Winter Swans' (Cluster 1 Unit 13) or 'The Charge of the Light Brigade' (Cluster 2 Unit 5).

Most of the poems are written to explore ideas and feelings related to the ups and downs of daily life – a lover's tiff in 'Neutral Tones' (Cluster 1 Unit 5) and a frightening childhood experience in the extract from 'The Prelude' (Cluster 2 Unit 3). Some take a passionate stance in relation to ideas and principles, such as 'Love's Philosophy' (Cluster 1 Unit 2) and 'Checking Out Me History' (Cluster 2 Unit 15), while others celebrate the achievements and dignity of ordinary people doing what they think best, such as 'Mother, any distance' (Cluster 1 Unit 11) and 'Kamikaze' (Cluster 2 Unit 14).

Whatever the kind of poem, one thing is clear. The writer will have had some purpose in writing it. This could be a **private** and **personal** purpose, like wanting to get some misery off their chest, or to confess feelings of regret, loss or a guilty conscience. Others may have a more **public** purpose, to make the reader think or feel something about the world around them. Both kinds of poems may have a purpose of changing people's perceptions of life and may be political or philosophical, for example 'London' (Cluster 2 Unit 2), or reflecting on private events and memories, for example 'Walking Away' (Cluster 1 Unit 7) or 'The Emigrée' (Cluster 2 Unit 13).

So, poetry can be narrative, dramatic, speculative, impressionistic, descriptive or argumentative. In all this mix, there is something for everyone.

CLUSTER 1

Love and relationships
1 When We Two Parted

GETTING STARTED – THE POEM AND YOU

This poem concerns the ending of a relationship and the response of someone who feels that they have been badly treated.

If you had been badly let down by someone, what would you do? For example would you be tempted to make your feelings public on social media? Would there be an element of revenge?

GETTING CLOSER – FOCUS ON DETAILS

First impressions

1 Now read the poem. It raises some questions: Who is he talking about? What has happened? How much do we know or can we deduce at this stage?

Create a table to help you tease out what you know. For example:

What you know or deduce	How you know it
A relationship has ended	
It took place a long time ago	'To sever for years'
	'Thy vows are all broken'
Their relationship was a secret	
The writer is bitter	

2 If you could give the poem another title, what would it be?

3 **Annotate** a copy of the poem in order to begin organising your thoughts about it. For example:

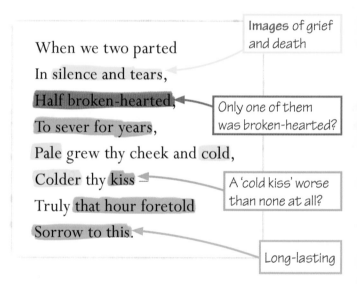

When we two parted
In silence and tears,
Half broken-hearted,
To sever for years,
Pale grew thy cheek and cold,
Colder thy kiss —
Truly that hour foretold
Sorrow to this.

Images of grief and death

Only one of them was broken-hearted?

A 'cold kiss' worse than none at all?

Long-lasting

Contexts

Lord Byron (1788–1824) was an English poet and one of the most famous members of the Romantic movement. This poem is said to be about his love affair with Lady Frances Webster. Not only was she a married woman, but she was also the wife of one of his friends. Later, after their affair ended, Byron learned of Lady Frances' new affair with the Duke of Wellington.

There are plenty of books and websites that will give you more information on the life and loves of Byron, about whom it was famously said that he was 'Mad, bad and dangerous to know'!

WHEN WE TWO PARTED

When we two parted
   In silence and tears,
Half broken-hearted,
   To sever for years,
Pale grew thy cheek and cold,   5
   Colder thy kiss —
Truly that hour foretold
   Sorrow to this.

The dew of the morning
   Sunk chill on my brow —   10
It felt like the warning
   Of what I feel now.
Thy vows are all broken,
   And light is thy fame;
I hear thy name spoken,   15
   And share in its shame.

They name thee before me —
   A knell to mine ear;
A shudder comes o'er me —
   Why wert thou so dear?   20
They know not I knew thee,
   Who knew thee too well;
Long, long shall I rue thee,
   Too deeply to tell.

In secret we met,   25
   In silence I grieve
That thy heart could forget,
   Thy spirit deceive.
If I should meet thee
   After long years,   30
How should I greet thee?
   With silence and tears.

Lord Byron

fame (14): reputation
knell (18): the sound of a
bell, especially when rung
for a death or funeral
rue (23): regret bitterly

 Listen to the poem on Cambridge Elevate

PUTTING DETAILS TO USE

Interpreting themes, ideas, attitudes and feelings

1 In pairs or small groups, look at the following table. The left-hand column contains certain lines from the poem and the right-hand column shows different ways to **interpret** these lines. Discuss which interpretations you think are the most appropriate. There is not necessarily a right and wrong answer – but you do have to agree on a choice.

'The dew of the morning Sunk chill on my brow – It felt like the warning Of what I feel now.'	The morning dew was: • like a cold sweat, an omen of the suffering to follow • cold, like your feelings and a sign of the chill that was to follow in my life • like a premonition of death.
'Thy vows are all broken, And light is thy fame;'	You've broken promises and: • your reputation is in tatters • your behaviour is well known • you are talked about everywhere.
'I hear thy name spoken, And share in its shame.'	• I can't bear to hear you talked about. • I feel ashamed of my association with you. • I'm embarrassed when people speak about what you're up to.
'They name thee before me – A knell to mine ear;'	I overhear people talking about you and to me it is like: • a funeral bell • the sound of death • a foretaste of death.
'A shudder comes o'er me –'	It makes me: • shiver in horror • shake with sadness • convulse with despair.
'They know not I knew thee, Who knew thee too well;'	• I knew you far better than they think. • I wish I had not known you so well. • They are ignorant of your true nature.
'Long, long shall I rue thee, Too deeply to tell.'	I regret: • ever knowing you • that we parted • that you broke your promises.

2 Share your decisions with the rest of the class. Do other groups disagree with some of your interpretations? If so, try to examine why.

They name thee before me –
A knell to mine ear;
A shudder comes o'er me –
Why wert thou so dear?

Learning checkpoint

Choose three extracts from the poem and give your response to them, each time beginning your response with 'Reading between the lines …' For example:

*In the second **verse** he says that he will regret ever knowing her for a very long time and these feelings of hurt are too deep to speak of. Reading between the lines and knowing something of his character, I feel that he is exaggerating how long it will take to get over her. Also, he is expressing his feelings in the poem so they are not too deep 'to tell' after all.*

Show your skills

Although the **rhythm** of the first verse is slightly irregular, the poem then settles down to a very clear beat. Read verses two and three aloud with a partner in a way that emphasises the regular beat:

The **dew** of the **morn**ing / Sank **chill** on my **brow**

Such a reading begins to sound very monotonous. Now experiment with reading those verses in a very different way. It may help to mark the lines with places where you intend to pause or to raise or lower the volume. You can decide your own abbreviations; this example uses the following: *italics* = quieter; // = pause (/// = longer pause); **bold** = louder; <u>underline</u> = slowing down.

The dew of the morning sank *chill on my brow*. // It felt like the **warning** /// of what <u>I feel now</u>.

Reading the poem in your own way will show that you have understood the importance of different words and phrases and are able to interpret them (and explain your choices). If possible, record your reading.

GETTING IT INTO WRITING

From the work you have done already, you should now be able to tackle a longer piece of writing about the poem. Answer the following question:
What are Byron's feelings about the parting and how well do you think he expresses them?

Here are some of the aspects you should consider:

- Byron's vocabulary – which words establish a particular feeling or **tone**?
- The **structure** of the poem – does the verse **form** and rhythm influence the way the poem makes you feel?
- The argument – how he builds up a case against the woman.
- The overall impact – do his words convince you? Do you think his reaction is typical?

Comparing poems

As you read the other poems in this collection, look out for similarities and differences between them. Sometimes their form (the way they are constructed, perhaps with formal verse patterns) will be very different, but their themes and points of view may be similar.

GETTING CREATIVE

Here is the first verse, expanded with the addition of some extra words and phrases to create a version from the woman's point of view. Choose another verse to adapt in a similar way. Here and there you may wish to change the word order, but try to stick to the original order as far as possible.

> *When we two parted, it was in silence and there were tears, of course. I was only half in love with you and could not pretend to be broken-hearted. It was not so hard to sever the ties. I had known you for years and knew your faults. Your cheek grew pale and cold, colder than the touch of your hand. Your parting kiss was truly the end, for it tasted of bitterness. I knew that hour that I had done the right thing. Our relationship only foretold sorrow. 'Yes, it's come to this,' I said.*

Your response

How would you feel if you received a message such as 'When We Two Parted?' Would you feel angry/resentful/remorseful/amused/irritated? How do you think the woman about whom the poem was written felt when she read it? You could write her reply!

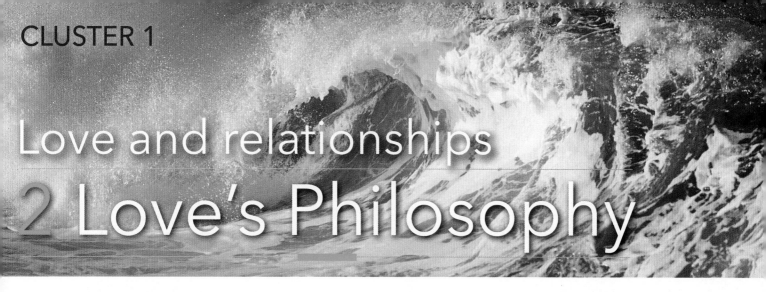

Love and relationships
2 Love's Philosophy

GETTING STARTED – THE POEM AND YOU

Read 'Love's Philosophy'. Do you think it is written seriously or is it a bit of light-hearted entertainment? How might the woman respond to this kind of persuasion?

Contexts

Percy Bysshe Shelley (1792-1822) was, like his friend Lord Byron, one of the most important Romantic poets. He made himself unpopular with some of his ideas on subjects such as atheism, vegetarianism and the need for social and political change, which at the time were controversial. This simple love poem shows a different, more personal side to Shelley, who usually wrote about more serious subjects such as politics.

GETTING CLOSER – FOCUS ON DETAILS

First impressions

1 The poem has a clear form, the second verse taking exactly the same pattern as the first. Read the poem aloud and then discuss these points with a partner:

   a How do the last lines of each verse differ from the rest of the poem?

   b In what ways does line 8 differ from line 16?

   c What is the effect of these shorter lines on the reader?

2 Can you spot any other kinds of repeated patterns in the poem? (Hint: Look at the position of verbs and nouns.)

Interpreting themes, ideas, attitudes and feelings

1 Natural forces and features are used throughout the poem. Make a list of them and the verbs that link them.

2 Look at the list of verbs you have written. These are not words that you would normally associate with rivers, mountains and so on. What associations do they have? (For example he uses 'mingle' twice, which has associations of being so closely mixed as to become inseparable.)

3 Whatever answers you came up with, it is likely that you associated Shelley's choice of verbs with human actions and feelings, not those of the landscape or weather. This demonstrates clearly how much he uses the technique of **personification**. The human element is left to the end of each verse: Why can't my spirit mingle with yours? Why not kiss me? After all the references to landscape, wind and weather, the final line comes down to earth with a bump! And as you have already noticed, this is where the line length and rhythm changes sharply, too. Shelley clearly wants the last line to have an impact.

What do you think is the effect of that last line? Does it make you laugh – or impress you with its urgency?

LOVE'S PHILOSOPHY

The fountains mingle with the river
    And the rivers with the ocean,
The winds of heaven mix for ever
    With a sweet emotion;
Nothing in the world is single;   5
    All things by a law divine
In one spirit meet and mingle.
    Why not I with thine? —

See the mountains kiss high heaven
    And the waves clasp one another;   10
No sister-flower would be forgiven
    If it disdained its brother;
And the sunlight clasps the earth
    And the moonbeams kiss the sea:
What is all this sweet work worth   15
    If thou kiss not me?

Percy Bysshe Shelley

---
fountains (1): springs

Listen to the poem on Cambridge Elevate

PUTTING DETAILS TO USE

1 Reread the poem and then decide which of these statements best describes Shelley's 'philosophy' – the argument he puts forward in the poem. If none of them fit closely with what you think, add your own or edit one of the statements:

a   All of these natural things meet and mingle, therefore we should also.
b   All things in nature mix naturally, so why shouldn't we do the same?
c   A divine law forces all things to blend together, so we must also do so.
d   The forces of nature are meaningless to me unless you give in to my desires.

2 Compare your choice with a partner and then share them with your class. The aim is to come up with a satisfactory one-line summary of Shelley's 'philosophy'.

3 Now work through the poem and decide, point by point, whether you agree with Shelley's argument. The table has been started, but feel free to change what has been put in so far:

'The fountains mingle with the river And the rivers with the ocean,'	Yes, they can be said to do this.
'The winds of heaven mix for ever With a sweet emotion;'	Winds don't necessarily mix – and they definitely don't show any sweet emotion.
'Nothing in the world is single;'	Some things are single, for example …
'All things by a law divine In one spirit meet and mingle. Why not I with thine? –'	No, all things do not …
'See the mountains kiss high heaven And the waves clasp one another;' 'No sister-flower would be forgiven If it disdained its brother; And the sunlight clasps the earth And the moonbeams kiss the sea: What is all this sweet work worth If thou kiss not me?'	If 'heaven' is the sky, then …

See the mountains kiss high heaven

Learning checkpoint

Write a few sentences describing Shelley's argument and then give your own response, exploring how far you find it convincing.

Show your skills

Look at the following response to 'Love's Philosophy' and see how far the writer has understood Shelley's argument and examined it critically. You could use a highlighter on a copy to mark the following aspects:

Gives evidence from the text
Describes accurately
Shows understanding
Explores critically

A couple of examples have already been done.

Shelley gives a number of examples of how things in the natural world meet and mingle, such as rivers into the sea and he maintains that there is a 'divine' law making this happen. In the second verse he goes further, saying that the mountains actually 'kiss' the heavens and the sunlight 'clasps the earth'. If all this is so, he says, why should not his spirit mingle with hers? He is going so far as to suggest that it is unnatural if they do not physically meet and, in the final lines, says that all the 'sweet work' of nature is meaningless to him if she will not kiss him. This seems like the argument of a desperate man, as there are so many faults in what he says. Even if it is natural that all things meet and mingle, why should she choose to do so with him rather than with someone else?

GETTING IT INTO WRITING

Comparing poems

'Love's Philosophy' depends on images from nature to convey the strength of the poet's feelings. As you work through the other poems in this collection, notice which ones draw upon nature or natural images in order to communicate the writer's feelings.

GETTING CREATIVE

Personification

Try out these tasks, all of which use the same technique as Shelley. (You will see that it is the verbs that do the personifying.)

a Write three or more examples of nature personified showing the closeness of the two aspects. For example: *The stream hugged the riverbank.*

b Write three or more examples of nature personified but showing the opposite. For example: *The waves gnawed ravenously at the shingle beach.* (Here the adverb helps the verb to seem even more 'human'.)

c Write three or more examples of inanimate (not living) objects personified. For example: *The motorbike snarled into life.*

d Personification is often achieved through the use of a **simile**. For example: *The vines clung to the tree like the arms of a drowning person.* Write three or more like this.

You will see that this simple technique can be a powerful tool for a poet - or indeed for any writer. Look out for it when you are reading; it crops up everywhere - quite often in sports writing.

Your response

Now that you've studied the poem in detail, what do you think of it? Is it presenting a 'serious' argument? Perhaps you think it is emotional blackmail dressed up in poetic words? Or is it just a bit of fun?

Love and relationships
3 Porphyria's Lover

GETTING STARTED – THE POEM AND YOU

As civilised and advanced human beings, we are nevertheless intrigued and fascinated by gruesome stories. Can you think of a recent news story that had a grisly or shocking element? Why do we want to hear about such things?

Which of these statements do you agree with?

a   It makes us feel better because it's happened to someone else.
b   It adds spice to an otherwise boring day.
c   There's something macabre in all of us.
d   I don't enjoy hearing about such things – it's sick.
e   It's a way of dealing with our own fears.
f   If it happened to someone we knew, we would feel differently.

GETTING CLOSER – FOCUS ON DETAILS

First impressions

Now read the poem or listen to it carefully.

Why? This is the question everyone asks about 'Porphyria's Lover'. Before you consider that question, make sure you have got the story clear in your head. Arrange the following events into **chronological** order:

> He opens her eyes.

> He rests her head on his shoulder.

> He strangles her with her own hair.

> He sits with her all night.

> He wonders what to do, then decides.

> Porphyria arrives.

> Porphyria's lover waits in the cottage.

> She covers his face with her hair.

> She tells him she loves him.

> She speaks but he does not reply.

> She takes off her wet outer clothes.

> She sits next to him and rests his head on her shoulder.

> The weather is stormy.

Interpreting themes, ideas, attitudes and feelings

1 Apart from the description of what happens, the **narrative**, we have only the lover's thoughts. Use a highlighter on a copy of the poem to mark his thoughts rather than any actions.

2 What clues are there as to why he kills her? Focus on the parts of the poem you have marked and discuss with a partner any possible motivations. Jot down your thoughts in preparation for the next activity.

PORPHYRIA'S LOVER

The rain set early in tonight,
 The sullen wind was soon awake,
It tore the elm-tops down for spite,
 and did its worst to vex the lake:
 I listened with heart fit to break.   5
When glided in Porphyria; straight
 She shut the cold out and the storm,
And kneeled and made the cheerless grate
 Blaze up, and all the cottage warm;
 Which done, she rose, and from her form 10
Withdrew the dripping cloak and shawl,
 And laid her soiled gloves by, untied
Her hat and let the damp hair fall,
 And, last, she sat down by my side
 And called me. When no voice replied, 15
She put my arm about her waist,
 And made her smooth white shoulder bare
And all her yellow hair displaced,
 And, stooping, made my cheek lie there,
 And spread, o'er all, her yellow hair,   20
Murmuring how she loved me – she
 Too weak, for all her heart's endeavour,

To set its struggling passion free
 From pride, and vainer ties dissever,
 And give herself to me for ever.   25
But passion sometimes would prevail,
 Nor could tonight's gay feast restrain
A sudden thought of one so pale
 For love of her, and all in vain:
 So, she was come through wind and rain. 30
Be sure I looked up at her eyes
 Happy and proud; at last I knew
Porphyria worshipped me; surprise
 Made my heart swell, and still it grew
 While I debated what to do.   35
That moment she was mine, mine, fair,
 Perfectly pure and good: I found
A thing to do, and all her hair
 In one long yellow string I wound

Listen to the poem on Cambridge Elevate

Three times her little throat around,   40
And strangled her. No pain felt she;
 I am quite sure she felt no pain.
As a shut bud that holds a bee,
 I warily oped her lids: again
 Laughed the blue eyes without a stain. 45
And I untightened next the tress
 About her neck; her cheek once more
Blushed bright beneath my burning kiss:
 I propped her head up as before,
 Only, this time my shoulder bore   50

Her head, which droops upon it still:
 The smiling rosy little head,
So glad it has its utmost will,
 That all it scorned at once is fled,
 And I, its love, am gained instead!   55
Porphyria's love: she guessed not how
 Her darling one wish would be heard.
And thus we sit together now,
 And all night long we have not stirred,
 And yet God has not said a word!   60

Robert Browning

PUTTING DETAILS TO USE

1 There are many interpretations of this poem. Have a class debate on opposing interpretations, for example:

He is a homicidal maniac *vs.* **There's more to it than that**

One half of the class should prepare arguments to support the idea that the lover is insane, and kills for reasons that are incomprehensible to sane people. The other half, though perhaps admitting that he is unbalanced, should look for some kind of reasoning - saving her from something, fulfilling her wishes or something else?

Use the internet to explore the many different theories about the poem. All these theories will have used evidence in the text to back them up. This is exactly what you have to do, too - and the main source for evidence will be those lines that you marked earlier. Examine them closely as if at a crime scene… For example:

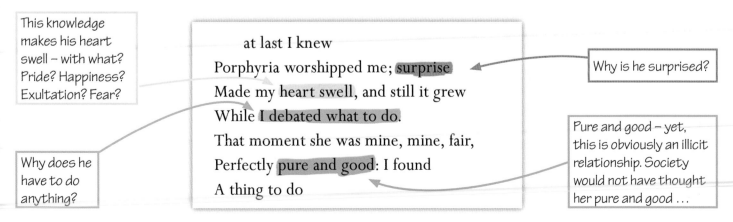

This knowledge makes his heart swell – with what? Pride? Happiness? Exultation? Fear?

Why is he surprised?

Why does he have to do anything?

Pure and good – yet, this is obviously an illicit relationship. Society would not have thought her pure and good …

at last I knew
Porphyria worshipped me; surprise
Made my heart swell, and still it grew
While I debated what to do.
That moment she was mine, mine, fair,
Perfectly pure and good: I found
A thing to do

Dramatic monologue

The term '**dramatic monologue**' is given to a poem that is dramatic (tells a good story) and is spoken by one (*mono*) person (in the same way that a **dialogue** is spoken by two or more people).

Dramatic monologues were not very common in Victorian poems and many readers at the time were confused by the fact that the poem is a **first-person narrative** and yet the 'I' is not Browning himself. Think back over other poems you have read in this collection. You can usually be sure that the 'I' refers to the poet. (Compare this with novels and short stories; they are often written in the first person but no one expects them to represent the thoughts and actions of the writer.)

2 The problem with this kind of poem is that you cannot know how far to trust what the character is saying. Work with a partner to find two pieces of evidence in the text that the narrator could be seen to be either lying or deluded.

 Contexts

Robert Browning (1812–1889) became one of the most popular Victorian poets. He tried writing plays, but soon realised that he was better at writing poetry. He is best known for his dramatic monologues, like this one – poems that tell a story, written in character. This is a rather creepy poem in which the narrator calmly murders his lover and then stays with her all night. The woman is named after a disease, porphyria, which can cause madness. This may be a clue to the state of mind of the poem's narrator. Insanity came to be a frequent subject of Browning's poetry.

He married the poet Elizabeth Barrett in secret, against her father's wishes, and they went to live in Italy until her death 15 years later. (See 'I think of thee!' in Unit 4.)

Show your skills

Look at the following piece of writing. Assess how far it shows evidence of:

* understanding the text
* a personal response to the text
* providing textual support for argument
* developing ideas or interpretations.

Porphyria's lover is an 'unreliable narrator' who is trying to make excuses for what he has done. He says that Porphyria is pure and good and that she loves him – worships him even – but we only have his word for this. Perhaps she did not murmur how she loved him but that this was the last time they could meet like this in secret. That would give him a motive for murder, a crime of passion. It would explain why he 'debated what to do' and also the fact that his heart was fit to break before she arrived. He must have expected something of the kind and that is why he sat in silence. He suspected that she was going to break the news this evening. She is too weak, he thinks, to set her 'struggling passions free' and their illicit affair must end. Of course, the whole thing might be in his fevered imagination or a fantasy that he has – it may never have happened at all. In fact it didn't – it was all in Browning's mind!

I listened with heart fit to break. When glided in Porphyria

 Learning checkpoint

One of the main reasons this poem has fascinated people over the years is because there is no obvious answer to the question: **Why?** Can you think of other examples of enduring mysteries? If the mystery was solved, would we still be interested?

Write three or four sentences for someone who has not seen the poem. Explain briefly what it is about and why you think it has remained a popular poem.

GETTING IT INTO WRITING

Now present your interpretation of the poem. In 200–300 words give your response to the question: **Why does Browning's poem 'Porphyria's Lover' continue to fascinate readers?**

Comparing poems

As you have seen, the **viewpoint** in this poem is that of a man whose statements cannot be necessarily be trusted. As you work your way through the poems in this collection, think about which 'voices' you trust. Which do you distrust? This is a personal response but you should be able to **justify** your views.

Make brief notes to refer to in a class discussion, for example:

'When We Two Parted'	The writer is trying to justify himself and blame someone else, so is likely to be biased.
'Eden Rock' (see Unit 9)	The writer seems to be very straightforward, but he may not have remembered things accurately.

Your response

What do you make of the final line? Is the speaker gloating that he has not been punished, convincing himself that he has, in fact, done the right thing – or not?

Love and relationships
4 Sonnet 29 – 'I think of thee!'

GETTING STARTED – THE POEM AND YOU

This is a love poem from one poet, Elizabeth, to another, her husband Robert. It expresses unrestrained love without any of the fixations we have seen in the previous love poems in the collection. The way she expresses her feelings might seem quite complex, but the emotion is clear and straightforward.

Read the poem. This transparent expression of love is common in many songs. Can you think of some examples?

 Contexts

When Elizabeth Barrett (1806–1861) met and married Robert Browning (see 'Porphyria's Lover' in the previous unit and 'My Last Duchess' in Cluster 2 Unit 4) in 1845, she was already one of the most popular and successful writers in Britain. Her poetry was widely read both in Britain and America. After her secret marriage, her stern and disapproving father disowned her. Throughout her life she suffered from poor health, and she was often too weak to leave the house.

In her writing she supported controversial social reforms, such as the banning of child labour and the abolition of slavery. This **sonnet** is one of 44 that Elizabeth Barrett wrote during her romance with Browning. All of them are love poems addressed to him.

GETTING CLOSER – FOCUS ON DETAILS

First impressions

Browning's words are so closely packed and full of emotion that you may have found it hard to understand on a first reading. Look at the following version, which has a different word order and different punctuation:

I think of thee! My thoughts twine and bud about thee, just as wild vines about a tree put out broad leaves. Soon there's nought to see except the straggling green which hides the wood.

Yet O my palm-tree, let it be understood, I will not have my thoughts instead of thee. Thou art dearer, better rather, than mere thoughts.

Renew thy presence instantly! Rustle thy boughs and set thy trunk all bare as a strong tree should. Let these bands of greenery which insphere thee drop down heavily, burst, shatter everywhere!

In this deep joy to see and hear thee (and breathe within thy shadow a new air) I do not think of thee – I am too near thee.

The whole poem is based on one comparison, a **metaphor** that is kept up all the way through. (This is called an **extended metaphor**.) Her thoughts about him are like foliage growing around the trunk of a tree. He is the tree, encased by her thoughts.

Listen to the poem on Cambridge Elevate

SONNET 29 – 'I THINK OF THEE!'

I think of thee! – my thoughts do twine and bud
About thee, as wild vines, about a tree,
Put out broad leaves, and soon there's nought to see
Except the straggling green which hides the wood.
Yet, O my palm-tree, be it understood   5
I will not have my thoughts instead of thee
Who art dearer, better! Rather, instantly
Renew thy presence; as a strong tree should,
Rustle thy boughs and set thy trunk all bare,
And let these bands of greenery which insphere thee,   10
Drop heavily down, – burst, shattered, everywhere!
Because, in this deep joy to see and hear thee
And breathe within thy shadow a new air,
I do not think of thee – I am too near thee.

Elizabeth Barrett Browning

PUTTING DETAILS TO USE

Analysing language, form and structure

Browning chose to use the sonnet form for her love poems. Sonnets have 14 lines, each line having ten syllables with five stressed syllables. (This kind of rhythm is called **iambic pentameter**. An **iamb** is a di-DA beat and **pent** means 'five', as in **pent**agon. Simple really.)

'I **think** of **thee!** – my **thoughts** do **twine** and **bud**'

This is a clear example of the length of the line and the number of stressed beats.

The poet keeps to the iambic pentameter fairly closely throughout the poem. This sometimes results in a poem beginning to sound predictable and, possibly, monotonous. Browning avoids this by breaking up the lines in a number of places, with the punctuation forcing the reader to pause in the middle of a line.

1 A sonnet is usually divided into eight lines and six lines and expected to have a **volta** (a change of direction of some kind) after the eighth line. It may be that the first eight lines pose a question and the final six lines answer it – or the final six lines begin a counter-argument, a kind of 'Yes, but …'

Work with a partner to decide if there is a change of any kind around line 8/9 in this sonnet.

Learning checkpoint

What do you think of the metaphor of thoughts as encircling vines? Write a couple of sentences explaining why you think the image is a good idea or not.

Sometimes writers will expect a reader to understand more than is stated explicitly. This is especially the case if the writer is using sarcasm or **irony**. However, it is also possible that some **implicit** meanings are there without the writer being aware of them. In the case of this sonnet, we do not know how far the poet was aware of possible interpretations; in Victorian England, writers took care not to offend with overt references to anything remotely sexual. Yet it is hard to read the following lines without thinking there might be other meanings:

as a strong tree should,

Rustle thy boughs and set thy trunk all bare,

And let these bands of greenery which insphere thee,

Drop heavily down,

2 Take a closer look at the language choices the writer has made. Make a copy of the following table to explore ideas about the words and phrases in the first column and their aptness for the part they play in the poem. Add two words or phrases of your own choice to the bottom of the list.

'twine and bud'	
'wild vines'	
'straggling green'	Why has she chosen straggling? It suggests something untidy, unkempt …
'palm-tree'	
'rustle thy boughs'	
'insphere'	To surround in a sphere – but a tree trunk is not that shape …
'burst, shattered'	
'within thy shadow'	
'a new air'	

GETTING IT INTO WRITING

Now consolidate what you have learned into a longer piece of writing. Write a response to the following question in about 300 words: **How does Elizabeth Barrett Browning express her feelings about Robert in the sonnet? Is she, in your view, successful?**

This question asks you to think about the writer's **feelings** (what are they?) and how she tries to convey them (the way she uses **language**). It also asks your opinion about how well she does this. As a very rough guide, you might divide your answer into three paragraphs of about 100 words each.

Comparing poems

You have now have encountered a number of poems about romantic relationships, including 'Love's Philosophy' and 'When We Two Parted'. Choose one of these to compare with 'I think of thee!'. Start by arranging the two poems side by side so that you can make notes while viewing both of them.

When you have finished making these notes, divide them into sections (perhaps using a highlighter) that will cover different aspects, such as:

*   the form of each poem
*   use of language
*   imagery
*   tone
*   the writer's attitude
*   your response.

Having compared the different aspects of the two poems, finish off with a conclusion that links the two with an opinion of your own.

GETTING CREATIVE

Writing challenge

Write a few lines of Robert Browning's response to Elizabeth. It does not have to be a sonnet! It might begin:

Your thoughts surround but not as strangling vines,
More like the gentle fronds of tropic plants,
Which ...

Your response

Do you think a poem like 'I think of thee!' has anything to do with relationships in the modern world? Why, or why not?

Because, in this deep joy to see and hear thee
And breathe within thy shadow a new air,
I do not think of thee – I am too near thee.

Love and relationships
5 Neutral Tones

GETTING STARTED – THE POEM AND YOU

Relationships can be the source of pain as well as pleasure. Perhaps you know people who have experienced the loss of a friendship or the end of a relationship – or perhaps it has happened to you.

Read the poem. What is your first reaction – do you sympathise with him or think that he has dwelt too much on it over the years?

GETTING CLOSER – FOCUS ON DETAILS

1 The poem is not clear about what exactly happened. Make a list of the **facts**, starting with: *They stood by the pond. It was winter …*

2 What can you **deduce** from the poem? Again, continue the list: *The occasion was the end of the relationship. The writer felt deceived …*

3 The reader is left to fill in the gaps. We know that some 'words played between us' but we can only guess what they might have been. What do you think she might have said?

'I don't love you.'

'I want to end our engagement.'

'I'm seeing someone else.'

The suggestions above are not very original. Write some of your own – but try and keep to the tone of the poem.

Interpreting themes, ideas, attitudes and feelings

1 In your opinion, which line most clearly sums up Hardy's feelings about love?

2 These might be Hardy's thoughts, based very closely on the words in the poem:

> *Your eyes looked on me so differently. They were as cold as eyes that rove, seeking somewhere else to look. It was as if you were thinking over all the tedious riddles of years ago – things we've been over time and time again. And some words played between us to and fro just as before – but the more we spoke the more our love was lost.*

The poem does not tell us what the woman was thinking, but we can make some guesses, based on what is written in the poem. For example her thoughts might begin:

> *I looked at you but I could not see the person I used to know. You thought my eyes were cold but they were merely sad …*

Continue writing her thoughts. How will you interpret 'The smile on your mouth was the deadest thing', 'Alive enough to have strength to die', and 'a grin of bitterness swept thereby'?

NEUTRAL TONES

We stood by a pond that winter day,
And the sun was white, as though chidden of God,
And a few leaves lay on the starving sod;
   —They had fallen from an ash, and were gray.

Your eyes on me were as eyes that rove   5
Over tedious riddles of years ago;
And some words played between us to and fro
    On which lost the more by our love.

The smile on your mouth was the deadest thing
Alive enough to have strength to die;   10
And a grin of bitterness swept thereby
    Like an ominous bird a-wing....

Since then, keen lessons that love deceives,
And wrings with wrong, have shaped to me
Your face, and the God-curst sun, and a tree,   15
    And a pond edged with grayish leaves.

Thomas Hardy

chidden of (2): told off by
starving sod (3): arid soil
wrings (14): twists or squeezes

Listen to the poem on Cambridge Elevate

33

PUTTING DETAILS TO USE

Analysing language, form and structure

'Neutral' can mean 'not taking sides', but can also mean 'has no strong feeling' and therefore also 'has no strong colour'. 'Neutral tones' are dull colours that lack life. In Hardy's poem, something that sounds positive is often cancelled out by something negative, for example her 'smile' was the 'deadest thing'.

1 What other examples can you find of something positive in the poem being cancelled out by something negative?

2 The poem follows a regular form: four-line verses rhyming ABBA. The final line of each verse is indented, which draws attention to it. What else changes in the last line in verses two, three and four?

3 Experiment with different readings of the poem. In groups of four, decide what emotion you will try to convey, for example sadness, bitterness, anger, utter despair. Divide the lines up between you and practise your presentation. Pace your reading so that you do not waste the effect of your emotion too early on.

4 Listen to each group's reading, recording them if possible. Discuss which were the most effective and how far they seemed to be true to the tone of the poem.

Contexts

Poets often create descriptions of **setting** that match the situation and enhance the mood of characters – this is called **sympathetic background**.

Thomas Hardy (1840–1928) was initially more famous for his novels, such as *Tess of the d'Urbervilles*, than for his poetry. Hardy uses sympathetic background in many of his novels as well as in poems such as 'Neutral Tones': when tragedy strikes characters, the weather is often miserable, as if in sympathy with a character's mood.

Learning checkpoint

Write a few sentences exploring how Hardy's choice of words reflects his feelings. You might start: *Right from the beginning, the tone of the poem is cold and lacking in colour. Even the sun is …*

Show your skills

Now look at these examples and see if you can pick out where the writer has moved from understanding and explaining to exploring the text.

Right from the beginning, the tone of the poem is cold and lacking in colour. Even the sun is lacking in colour, being deathly white like the face of someone who has just been scolded or received a shock. Leaves are usually a sign of life, but here they are dead and lie grey on the bare earth. Anything that had life has now lost it and even the tree is an ash.

Smiles are usually a sign of happiness but here the smile is dead, as if there is no smile in her eyes and the smile on her mouth is false, or forced. He notes every detail of her expression so that she can hardly move without an attempt at a smile being turned into something bitter, with worse to come because it is as ominous as a bird of ill-omen, like a raven.

GETTING IT INTO WRITING

The cold note that is present throughout the poem turns to bitterness in the last verse:

Since then, keen lessons that love deceives,

And wrings with wrong, have shaped to me

Your face, and the God-curst sun, and a tree,

And a pond edged with grayish leaves.

1 Write the verse in the middle of a sheet of paper and add your thoughts and queries to it. This could be a group activity, using a large sheet of paper.

2 Using the notes as a starting point, write a full report on Hardy's state of mind as revealed in the final verse.

Comparing poems

There are similarities between this poem and Lord Byron's 'When We Two Parted'. Look closely at the language choices made by the poets in the two poems and make a list of similarities and differences. For example:

	'Neutral Tones'	'When We Two Parted'
Similarities	Both refer to coldness	
	'winter day, / And the sun was white,'	'cold, / Colder thy kiss'
Differences	Speaks of 'us' and 'our' but does not use 'I'	Does not refer to 'us' or 'our'. Uses 'thee' and 'I'

What can you deduce from the list you have made? (For example there is a greater sense of distance in Byron's poem, whereas Hardy seems to be clinging on to an idea of togetherness with his use of 'us' and 'our'.) Write four or five bullet points to explain your findings.

Your response

1 How much sympathy do you feel for Hardy (or the character he portrays)?

2 Is a picture worth a thousand words? Hardy paints a picture that is almost impressionist. The central characters are sketched with emotions given full attention; some background is filled in but the rest is left vague. How suitable do you think this image is as an illustration for the poem?

Using an image search and search words such as 'end of relationship', find a picture that you think illustrates the poem well. Be prepared to justify your choice.

Explore the poem further with a video activity on Cambridge Elevate

Love and relationships
6 The Farmer's Bride

GETTING STARTED – THE POEM AND YOU

Most of the poems in this collection directly express the personal experiences and feelings of the poet. 'The Farmer's Bride', like 'Porphyria's Lover', does not do this. Instead, the writer puts herself in someone else's situation. Interestingly, Charlotte Mew does not put herself in the situation of the bride but of the farmer: more challenging but more revealing.

How easy or hard do you think it is to imagine and convey what someone else might be feeling?

GETTING CLOSER – FOCUS ON DETAILS

First impressions

1 Read 'The Farmer's Bride'. How would you describe the farmer? Some possible words are suggested, but add some of your own. Arrange them in order of their suitability.

frustrated	plain-speaking	worried
impatient	thoughtless	rough
amazed	unimaginative	kind
disturbed	perplexed	sad

2 Find evidence in the poem to support the three adjectives you found most suitable in your response to the previous question.

Interpreting themes, ideas, attitudes and feelings

How far does knowing about a writer help us to understand or appreciate their work? Some would argue that it doesn't matter if we don't know the details of a writer's life: it's the words on the page that should be judged. Others would say that the **context** is important in understanding a piece of writing, including knowledge of the writer and of the time and place in which the text was created.

1 You have gathered a first impression of 'The Farmer's Bride'. Now read something about the writer.

 Contexts

Charlotte Mew's life (1869–1928) was full of sadness and tragedy. There was mental illness in her family, and two of her six brothers and sisters spent their lives in an asylum. Three others died young. She wrote poetry and stories in which death, mental illness and loneliness are common themes. Although her work was admired by important writers such as Thomas Hardy, Siegfried Sassoon and Virginia Woolf, she was not very popular in her lifetime, and remained very poor. After the death of her last remaining sibling, she took her own life. Her character can perhaps be summed up by her reply to the question 'Are you Charlotte Mew?'. She replied 'I am sorry to say that I am'.

 Read a longer biography of Charlotte Mew on the Poetry Foundation website

THE FARMER'S BRIDE

Three Summers since I chose a maid,
Too young maybe – but more's to do
At harvest-time than bide and woo.
    When us was wed she turned afraid
Of love and me and all things human;   5
Like the shut of a winter's day
Her smile went out, and 'twasn't a woman –
    More like a little frightened fay.
        One night, in the Fall, she runned away.

'Out 'mong the sheep, her be,' they said,   10
Should properly have been abed;
But sure enough she wasn't there
Lying awake with her wide brown stare.
    So over seven-acre field and up-along
        across the down
We chased her, flying like a hare   15
Before our lanterns. To Church-Town
    All in a shiver and a scare
We caught her, fetched her home at last
    And turned the key upon her, fast.

She does the work about the house   20
As well as most, but like a mouse:
    Happy enough to chat and play
    With birds and rabbits and such as they,
    So long as men-folk keep away.
'Not near, not near!' her eyes beseech   25
When one of us comes within reach.
    The women say that beasts in stall
    Look round like children at her call.
    I've hardly heard her speak at all.

Shy as a leveret, swift as he,   30
Straight and slight as a young larch tree,
Sweet as the first wild violets, she,
To her wild self. But what to me?

The short days shorten and the oaks are
        brown,
    The blue smoke rises to the low grey sky,   35
One leaf in the still air falls slowly down,
    A magpie's spotted feathers lie
On the black earth spread white with rime,
The berries redden up to Christmas-time.
    What's Christmas-time without there be   40
    Some other in the house than we!

She sleeps up in the attic there
    Alone, poor maid. 'Tis but a stair
Betwixt us. Oh! my God! the down,
The soft young down of her, the brown,   45
The brown of her – her eyes, her hair, her
    hair!

Charlotte Mew

bide (3): stay somewhere
woo (3): make someone
love and (usually) marry you
fay (8): fairy
leveret (30): young hare

🔊 Listen to the poem on Cambridge Elevate

2 Which of the following statements do you agree with most strongly? Why?
Select a statement and write a sentence to explain why you have chosen it.
You can write your own statement if you wish.

a It's helpful to know about Mew's life.
b It's unnecessary to know about her life.
c It's confusing to know about her life.
d It's very revealing to know about her life.

When you are thinking about answers to the question 'Why?' you may wish to
use or adapt one of these explanations:

e because it adds depth to an understanding of the poem
f because the poem tells a story which is complete in itself
g because we start thinking about her rather than the people in the poem
h because it makes us see the themes of the poem in a slightly different way.

PUTTING DETAILS TO USE

Analysing language, form and structure

1 Look more closely at Mew's choice of language. Pick six words or phrases that you think are worth
commenting on and explore Mew's use of them. For example you may want to think about:

a similes
b **alliteration** (for example look at lines 30–33)
c repetition of certain words (for example 'brown').

2 There are many references to time passing and the seasons turning in the poem. Find at least five
examples. Why do you think the poet chose to include so many of these?

 Learning checkpoint

Although the title is 'The Farmer's Bride', the poem tells us as much about the farmer as his
bride. How does Mew indicate aspects of his character and feelings without describing them
directly? For example:

"twasn't a woman" 'she runned away'	He speaks in a rural **dialect**, implying that he is a plain, working man.
'more's to do … than bide and woo'	He offers an excuse for choosing someone who is really too young.

Now do the same for the bride, using both the farmer's description of her and reading between
the lines of what he says.

Sweet as the first wild violets, she, To her wild self. But what to me?

Show your skills

You have now looked at the poem quite closely – and there is a lot to see! Look at this annotation of verse two:

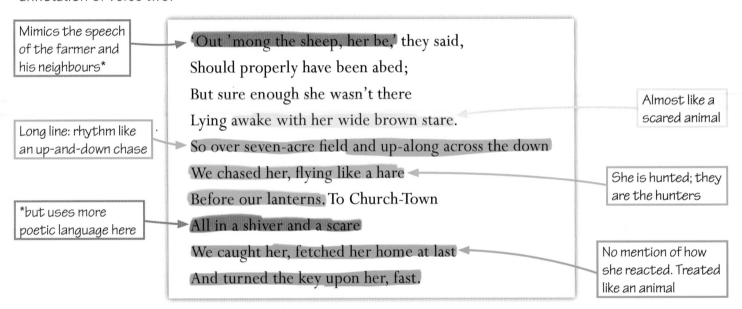

Mimics the speech of the farmer and his neighbours*

Long line: rhythm like an up-and-down chase

*but uses more poetic language here

'Out 'mong the sheep, her be,' they said,
Should properly have been abed;
But sure enough she wasn't there
Lying awake with her wide brown stare.
So over seven-acre field and up-along across the down
We chased her, flying like a hare
Before our lanterns. To Church-Town
All in a shiver and a scare
We caught her, fetched her home at last
And turned the key upon her, fast.

Almost like a scared animal

She is hunted; they are the hunters

No mention of how she reacted. Treated like an animal

These notes were used to create the following commentary, which has a high level of analysis. See if you can spot where the writer moves from description to more detailed analysis – and where ideas are explored that are only hinted at in the text itself:

Mew uses words like 'runned' and 'her be' to mimic the speech of country folk, which does give a sense of place and time, but she doesn't stick to it. Quite soon she is writing in more poetic ways with phrases like 'all in a shiver and a stare' and this is true throughout the poem. There is a regular pattern to the verse but she varies it for effect, for example in line 5 where the line is longer and seems to echo the chase over the uneven countryside. This is emphasised by all the prepositions 'over up along across down' tumbling over each other. When Mew describes the girl (through the farmer's eyes), she is seen like an animal (perhaps scared or trapped) with her 'wide brown stare' and she is hunted down and then imprisoned like an animal. There is no mention, in spite of the writer being female, of her feelings – but if she was frightened and hesitant before, she will be even more so now!

GETTING IT INTO WRITING

Now take any of the longer verses and write your own commentary. Be adventurous enough to explore your own ideas and interpretations, always bearing in mind that they should be anchored at some point to words in the text!

Comparing poems

The **persona** of the farmer in 'The Farmer's Bride' tells his sad story and describes his bride but in doing so he reveals a good deal about himself. In which other poems do you find the writer or narrator revealing his or her own character when writing about someone else? Pick one in particular and be prepared to explain why you have chosen that poem and what you think it reveals about the narrator.

Alternatively, if you would like to look at a unfamiliar poem to gain practice for the 'unseen poetry' section of your exam, 'My Last Duchess' by Robert Browning (see Cluster 2 Unit 4) would make an interesting comparison when thinking about this.

GETTING CREATIVE

Charlotte Mew did voluntary social work in London but there would have been no social workers in the countryside where this poem is set. The local vicar would be the only person who might possibly take an interest.

Imagine the vicar's wife has visited, having heard about this strange young bride and spoken not only to the farmer but also, eventually, to the girl. Write her impressions, using the form of a diary entry or a conversational report to her husband.

Your response

Do you think Charlotte Mew has created a fictional situation or written about someone she knew?

How successful is she in putting herself into the situation of a male – and a farmer?

So over seven-acre field and up-along across the down
We chased her, flying like a hare

Love and relationships
7 Walking Away

GETTING STARTED – THE POEM AND YOU

1 In this poem, the writer is remembering his son playing his first game of football and then going off to school.

    a What is your first memory of school? How did you feel?
    b How do you think your parents felt about you going off to school?

2 The poem might contain some unfamiliar words. Choose a word or phrase from the word clouds that you feel best defines the following words from the poem:

    a gait
    b touch-lines
    c pathos
    d eddying
    e selfhood
    f irresolute
    g half-fledged.

wrinkles • entrance • sides of a playing area • sinking • flying • individual character • way of walking • sorrow • selfishness • soft • wavering • grief • foolishness • whirling • limp • babyish • unique identity • indecisive • nearly ready to fly

ℹ Contexts

Cecil Day-Lewis (1904–1972) is best remembered for being the Poet Laureate of Great Britain (a title awarded by the Queen) for the last few years of his life. He also wrote detective stories under the pseudonym Nicholas Blake.

'Walking Away' is one of his best-known poems, and is about his son, Sean. In the poem, he is thinking back to when Sean started at boarding school at the age of seven. His other (younger) son is the famous Oscar-winning actor Daniel.

WALKING AWAY

It is eighteen years ago, almost to the day –
A sunny day with the leaves just turning,
The touch-lines new-ruled – since I watched you play
Your first game of football, then, like a satellite
Wrenched from its orbit, go drifting away   5

Behind a scatter of boys. I can see
You walking away from me towards the school
With the pathos of a half-fledged thing set free
Into a wilderness, the gait of one
Who finds no path where the path should be.   10

That hesitant figure, eddying away
Like a winged seed loosened from its parent stem,
Has something I never quite grasp to convey
About nature's give-and-take – the small, the scorching
Ordeals which fire one's irresolute clay.   15

I have had worse partings, but none that so
Gnaws at my mind still. Perhaps it is roughly
Saying what God alone could perfectly show –
How selfhood begins with a walking away,
And love is proved in the letting go.   20

Cecil Day-Lewis

 Listen to the poem on Cambridge Elevate

PUTTING DETAILS TO USE

1 To get an overall idea of the poem, try making a summary of each verse. For example:

It is eighteen years ago, almost to the day –
A sunny day with the leaves just turning,
The touch-lines new-ruled – since I watched you play
Your first game of football, then, like a satellite
Wrenched from its orbit, go drifting away

> *The poet recalls the day he saw his son play his first game of football and then go away.*

2 Share these with a partner and then in larger groups. It should be possible to reach a general level of agreement. Which lines seems to be the most difficult to agree on? As a class, with guidance from your teacher, try to resolve any problem areas.

 Learning checkpoint

What have you discovered about the poem so far? Write two or three sentences in answer to each of these questions:

a What is the event described in the poem?
b How does the writer feel about the event?
c What do you think about the relationship of the parent and the child?

Show your skills

Now think about how to use your notes to write something longer. You will need to show your reading skills. The following table shows some simple examples of how to do this. Turn five of your own notes into longer sentences using the sentence starter examples.

Reading skills to show in your writing	Examples of starting points
Understanding: understanding is a grasp of the basics of what the poem is about, which could be people, events, situations or places.	The writer remembers the day his son began school. In particular … He remembers feeling …
Interpreting themes, ideas, attitudes and feelings: when you interpret, you move from your understanding of the poem, to show what your understanding means to you or to someone else.	I think his feelings are more intense than many parents, because …
Exploring implied meanings: this is where you understand more than is obviously stated and you 'read between the lines'.	From the way he describes the boy leaving, I think the poet … On the other hand, the boy …

GETTING IT INTO WRITING

Now write a paragraph expressing in more detail what you believe the poem is about, together with your feelings about the way the poet has tried to convey his thoughts. You may wish to use or adapt this outline:

The poet recalls a memory of …

He remembers some specific things …

Most of all, though, he remembers …

He compares the way his son went away to …

The poet communicates an impression of his son as a …

He seems to think that …

Overall, I feel that the poem …

Comparing poems

Your work in this unit should have made you realise that the poem can evoke a number of reactions, from empathy with the father (or the son) – to your own more personal view (perhaps you think the father is overreacting, for example). Choose another poem from this cluster to compare how much you empathise (or not) with the narrator or another person in the poem.

Your response

- How would you describe the relationship between the writer and his son?
- Why do you think Day-Lewis wrote the poem?
- What do you think his son would think of the poem, now that he is grown up?

 Learning checkpoint

Here are two examples of student responses. Each has positive aspects. Read them carefully and make a note of parts you feel are beginning to explore the poem more deeply. Also note aspects where you think improvements could be made. Some notes have already been made on the first response.

The poet recalls a memory of the time when his son went to school and he had to watch him go and he was unhappy about it. He remembers some specific things like the leaves turning and the touch-lines new-ruled. Most of all, though, he remembers how his son walked away towards the school. He compares the way his son went away to a sad half-fledged thing. The poet communicates an impression of his son as someone who is a bit lost in his new surroundings. The poet's feelings about this event are sad. Overall, I feel that the poem puts across the father's feelings in a very descriptive way, even though he seems to think that he doesn't.

> Shows understanding

> 'unhappy' is a bit weak

> Shows interpretation of feelings

> Implied meanings

The poet recalls a memory of his son going off to school for the first time. He remembers some specific things very vividly, such as the leaves and the newly painted touch-lines. Most of all, though, he remembers the way his son went off with the other boys looking hesitant. He compares the way his son went away to a seed fluttering from a branch or a satellite being pulled out of its orbit. The poet communicates an impression of his son as a child who is not really ready to leave the nest and his feelings about this event are still powerful after many years. They 'gnaw at his mind' even though he has experienced worse partings. He seems to think that he is unable to express his feelings about needing to let go but he knows that letting go is necessary if the child is to be able to grow up. Overall, I feel that the poem does express the writer's feelings of loss quite well, though sometimes the way he puts things is not as straightforward as they could be.

CLUSTER 1
Love and relationships
8 Letters from Yorkshire

GETTING STARTED – THE POEM AND YOU

How is getting or sending a letter different from getting or sending a digital message? Have you ever sent or received a personal letter? What is the difference between getting a birthday or Christmas greeting by post and getting one electronically?

GETTING CLOSER – FOCUS ON DETAILS

First impressions

1 Now read 'Letters from Yorkshire'. When we read a piece of writing such as this, we tend to imagine the people involved, in this case, the writer of the letter and the person receiving it. What are the possibilities? Which seem most likely to you?

son or daughter brother or sister wife or husband friend lover grandparent grandson or granddaughter parent	getting a letter from	son or daughter brother or sister wife or husband friend lover grandparent grandson or granddaughter parent

2 'It's not romance, simply how things are' is a line that will have influenced your choices. What does it imply to you?

PUTTING DETAILS TO USE

Analysing language, form and structure

1 There is a **contrast** in the poem between closeness and distance, both physically and emotionally.

Using a copy of the poem, either on paper or an electronic version, mark the text to bring out these two aspects. For example: 'It's not romance' implies emotional distance, but the word 'heartful' implies the writer cares.

Contexts

Maura Dooley (born in 1957) has Irish roots, but was born in Cornwall, grew up in Bristol, lived in Yorkshire and then finally moved to London. She is a successful writer and a teacher. Several collections of her poems have been published. Her poetry is often simple and reflective, but the images she creates represent deep and complex feelings. This poem was inspired by letters she received from a friend which made her miss Yorkshire.

LETTERS FROM YORKSHIRE

In February, digging his garden, planting potatoes,
he saw the first lapwings return and came
indoors to write to me, his knuckles singing

as they reddened in the warmth.
It's not romance, simply how things are.   5
You out there, in the cold, seeing the seasons

turning, me with my heartful of headlines
feeding words onto a blank screen.
Is your life more real because you dig and sow?

You wouldn't say so, breaking ice on a waterbutt,   10
clearing a path through snow. Still, it's you
who sends me word of that other world

pouring air and light into an envelope. So that
at night, watching the same news in different houses,
our souls tap out messages across the icy miles.   15

Maura Dooley

Listen to the poem on Cambridge Elevate

2 Look at the personal pronouns in the poem:

he	his	his	me	me	me	my
our	they	you	you	you	your	

a Which pronoun is most obviously missing?

b Look at lines 6–13 and replace 'you' and 'your' with 'him/he' and 'his', making other adjustments as required. How does it change the tone of the poem?

Learning checkpoint

Write two or three sentences to explain why you think Dooley often uses 'you' and 'your' rather than 'him/he' and 'his'.

Show your skills

In the following examples, students have thought about the use of personal pronouns and about the overall tone of the poem. Look for signs that they have understood the gist of the poem, used some evidence and developed their thoughts beyond the obvious.

Maura Dooley is imagining him gardening and working outside while she is inside. As she thinks about him, he becomes more real to her and it is as if she is talking to him, not about him, because she shifts from 'he' to 'you'.

The poet envisages the man who has written to her as if she can see him. She uses 'you' because it brings him closer but she does not ever say 'I' when she is writing about herself. She talks of 'me' as if she was looking at herself from a distance, too.

Although they are far apart in distance and in what they are doing, the poet shows how close she feels by using 'you' instead of 'he'. She also shows how well she knows him through phrases such as 'You wouldn't say so' and the fact that she has seen him doing tasks such as breaking ice on the waterbutt.

GETTING IT INTO WRITING

1 Write a paragraph exploring the various contrasts and similarities that are either expressed or hinted at in the poem, for example he is outside while she is inside. You may want to make use of words and phrases such as:

whereas	however	on the other hand
although	in spite of	

2 What do you think the last line implies? Include a sentence at the end of your paragraph to explain your ideas.

our souls tap out messages
across the icy miles.

Comparing poems

This task asks you to compare Maura Dooley's poem with that of Cecil Day-Lewis. The following table will help you to bring out some of the main points. Some of the points have already been partly filled in – though you could alter them or disagree with them.

	Dooley	Day-Lewis	Evidence
Theme/topic		The theme is the poet's relationship with his son …	
Form/structure		The poem is written in long lines of …	
Language – vocabulary	The poet mostly uses everyday language except …		
Language – interesting features			'like a satellite / Wrenched from its orbit'
Tone	Conversational tone, as if she is talking to …		
Response		I can understand some of the poet's sadness at watching his son leave, but …	
Summary	The writer seems resigned to their separation and …		

Now take any two of the rows you have filled in and turn them into continuous **prose**.

GETTING CREATIVE

Using the same style and perhaps some of the same words, write from the **perspective** of the person who has been outside gardening. For example:

In March, tidying her desk, looking through the small window,
she saw the neighbours return from holiday and sat down
to write to me …

Your response

The poet asks the question 'Is your life more real because you dig and sow?' because she wonders if her life in a town or city, working with a computer screen, is somehow cut off from reality.

What do you feel about this – is urban life any less 'real' than rural life?

Love and relationships
9 Eden Rock

GETTING STARTED – THE POEM AND YOU

1 What memories do you have from childhood? In pairs, each pick one memory and in one minute describe it in as much detail as possible to the other person. Take a further minute each to ask follow-up questions in order to find out as much detail as possible.

2 Read the poem 'Eden Rock'. How old do you think the writer is in the scene the poem describes?

a   I think the writer is under five, because …

b   I think the writer is between five and seven, because …

c   I think the writer is older than seven, because …

ℹ Contexts

Charles Causley (1917–2003) was a quiet and modest man. He was born and brought up in Cornwall, where he lived for most of his life, and which he wrote about in many of his poems. His poetry is known for its simplicity and directness, often in the form of ballads – traditional narrative poems in short rhyming verses. Some of his poems were written for children. One of the best known of these is 'Timothy Winters', which you might like to read. 'Eden Rock' is one of several poignant poems that Causley wrote about his parents.

GETTING CLOSER – FOCUS ON DETAILS

First impressions

1 Does the scene described in the poem remind you of similar experiences – or does it seem remote and unfamiliar? Why?

2 There are some very precise details in the poem. Annotate a copy of the poem with notes that would explain these details to someone from another culture. For example:

> She pours tea from a Thermos,

A vacuum flask – known by the name of the maker, rather like ball pens are often called biros.

3 Why do you think the writer is deliberately reliving this experience? What might be his feelings as he does so?

4 The last line leaves the reader wondering what is meant by 'I had not thought that it would be like this'. What do you think the 'it' refers to? This is an important part of the poem, so – even if you're not sure – give it some thought.

EDEN ROCK

They are waiting for me somewhere beyond Eden Rock:
My father, twenty-five, in the same suit
Of Genuine Irish Tweed, his terrier Jack
Still two years old and trembling at his feet.

My mother, twenty-three, in a sprigged dress   5
Drawn at the waist, ribbon in her straw hat,
Has spread the stiff white cloth over the grass.
Her hair, the colour of wheat, takes on the light.

She pours tea from a Thermos, the milk straight
From an old H.P. Sauce bottle, a screw   10
Of paper for a cork; slowly sets out
The same three plates, the tin cups painted blue.

The sky whitens as if lit by three suns.
My mother shades her eyes and looks my way
Over the drifted stream. My father spins   15
A stone along the water. Leisurely,

They beckon to me from the other bank.
I hear them call, 'See where the stream-path is!
Crossing is not as hard as you might think.'

I had not thought that it would be like this.   20

Charles Causley

PUTTING DETAILS TO USE

Analysing language, form and structure

If you look a little closer at the words Causley has used, you will begin to see that there is more to the poem than just a description of a childhood event. Examine these words and phrases and see what you can deduce.

	What I think this implies	Questions I have
'In the same suit'		
'Still two years old'	The memory is from a time when his father's dog was still young	
'The same three plates'		
'Leisurely they beckon'	They are relaxed about the boy's safety	
'Crossing is not as hard as you might think'		Double meaning?
'I had not thought that it would be like this'		What does 'it' refer to?

Interpreting themes, ideas, attitudes and feelings

1 Imagine you are the boy in the poem, on one side of the river. How are you feeling and what are you thinking? What evidence from the poem suggests these thoughts to you?

2 Imagine you are the father or the mother, on the other side of the stream. How are you feeling and what are you thinking? What evidence from the poem suggests these thoughts to you?

3 Imagine you are the boy, now grown up, remembering. How are you feeling and what are you thinking? What evidence from the poem suggests these thoughts to you?

Learning checkpoint

Look again at these lines.

They beckon to me from the other bank.
I hear them call, 'See where the stream-path is!
Crossing is not as hard as you might think.'

I had not thought that it would be like this.

Using these lines as your starting point, explain what you think they add to the poem and what you feel the poem – taken as a whole – is about.

GETTING IT INTO WRITING

Show your skills

Now that you have made notes about the poem, you need to start thinking about how you can use them to write something longer. You will need to show your reading skills. The table shows some simple examples of how to do it. How would you end the sentences started in the table?

Reading skills to show in your writing	Example
Interrogating	Causley is reflecting on his connection to his parents and seeing the crossing of the stream as a symbol of ...
Analysing	The poet changes tense between the last two lines. He also leaves a gap. I think this is to show ...
Perspectives	The poem is about parent-child relationships and how they change over the years. Starting with the memory of the picnic, Causley goes on to ...

Comparing poems

The writer here is working in a similar way to how a painter might compose a picture. Reread the poem quietly and see if you can detect how Causley conveys an atmosphere of the place and the time. As well as the choice of words, think about the length and rhythm of the lines, the half-rhyme, the conversational tone.

Focusing on this aspect of the poem, which other poems in this cluster would work well to compare with 'Eden Rock'?

GETTING CREATIVE

1 Think of an event in your life that you can remember vividly. An event similar to a picnic or a trip to the country would be ideal, but it is not essential as long as it is outdoors. Run the event through in your mind as if it were a video clip. Now stop at the most important moment and focus on that – as if you had pressed the pause button. Now answer the following questions as simply as you can:

a   Where are you?
b   Who are you with?
c   What is the weather like?
d   What are you wearing?
e   What is your posture?
f   What are you carrying/holding/touching?
g   What can you see?
h   What can you hear?
i   What is your emotion?
j   Why is this moment important?

2 Use the answers to these questions to form a piece of writing. Do not be tempted to add too much to it as it is meant to be a snapshot of a moment. You could then rework your 'snapshot' into a piece of poetry.

Your response

Conversation is, usually, very different from the carefully considered words of a poem. How do you think Charles Causley might have spoken to someone close to him (a friend, his wife, children, for example) about this memory? For example:

'Did I ever tell you about that time when I was a kid and we had a picnic by the river ...'

How do you think he feels about his parents and his childhood?

Love and relationships
10 Follower

GETTING STARTED – THE POEM AND YOU

As in the poems 'Walking Away' and 'Eden Rock', this writer is also thinking back to childhood.

Seamus Heaney grew up in a farming community. His early experiences would be quite different from those of most of us.

1 How do you think a childhood on a farm might be different from one in a town or in the suburbs?

2 What do you think might be the positive aspects of a childhood like this?

3 What do you think might be the negative aspects?

> ### ⓘ Contexts
>
> Seamus Heaney (1939–2013) was one of the major poets of the 20th century. He won the Nobel Prize for Literature in 1995.
>
> He was the eldest of a large farming family in Northern Ireland. Many of his poems are about the past and about rural life and traditions. In this poem, he writes about coming to realise how skilled his father was, and seems troubled by the memory of him. Perhaps he feels guilty that he did not carry on the tradition, but instead became a poet, or feels unable to live up to his father's example.

GETTING CLOSER – FOCUS ON DETAILS

First impressions

Read 'Follower'. Which of the following best sums up the poem? Choose one summary and then discuss what has, nevertheless, been missed out.

a   As a boy, Heaney followed his father and was a hindrance to him as he ploughed.

b   Heaney used to follow his father around and get in his way, but now it is the other way around.

c   Heaney wanted to be a farmer like his father but became a writer instead.

d   Heaney admired his father's skills with the plough, but was more of a nuisance than a help.

Vocabulary

There are some words in the poem that you will probably not know. They are specific to ploughing and to a particular area of the country.

1 Make a copy of the following table to list the words you're unsure of. After some research or class discussion, fill in the third column.

Word	I think it might mean	I'm pretty sure it means

FOLLOWER

My father worked with a horse-plough,
His shoulders globed like a full sail strung
Between the shafts and the furrow.
The horses strained at his clicking tongue.

An expert. He would set the wing   5
And fit the bright steel-pointed sock.
The sod rolled over without breaking.
At the headrig, with a single pluck

Of reins, the sweating team turned round
And back into the land. His eye   10
Narrowed and angled at the ground,
Mapping the furrow exactly.

I stumbled in his hob-nailed wake,
Fell sometimes on the polished sod;
Sometimes he rode me on his back   15
Dipping and rising to his plod.

I wanted to grow up and plough,
To close one eye, stiffen my arm.
All I ever did was follow
In his broad shadow round the farm.   20

I was a nuisance, tripping, falling,
Yapping always. But today
It is my father who keeps stumbling
Behind me, and will not go away.

Seamus Heaney

Listen to the poem on Cambridge Elevate

2 Do you think it really matters if you don't know the exact meanings of some of the words? Discuss your ideas with a partner.

3 Apart from those few terms, the vocabulary used by the writer is familiar. Look at Heaney's use of nouns. In which verses are concrete nouns most frequent? Why do you think this is?

4 Now look at the poet's use of verbs. Highlight a copy of the poem, using one colour to mark verbs that describe the father's actions and another to mark verbs that describe the son's actions. Compare the two sets of verbs: what do you notice?

PUTTING DETAILS TO USE

1 This poem is full of striking contrasts or opposites. For example: father/son, skill/clumsiness. See how many examples you can find and make a note of them. Then compare your list with that of a partner and create a shared list. You may find that there are some very similar pairs, for example care/awkwardness, which is almost the same as skill/clumsiness, but keep both.

2 Share your pairs of opposites or contrasts with the rest of the class. Then, as a class, discuss which you think are the most important.

Show your skills

Write three or four sentences describing and explaining what you have noticed about the poem's use of contrasts. Try to move from simple understanding of the poem towards interpretation and **inferring** meaning. For example:

As a boy, Heaney felt that his father was skilful, an 'expert', while he was clumsy, a 'nuisance' who 'stumbled in his hob-nailed wake', but now …

Interpreting themes, ideas, attitudes and feelings

1 Now read the poem again and concentrate on the differences between the verses. The first three verses have a similar theme. What is it?

2 The theme changes with verse four and again in the following verse. How?

3 Finally, look at verse six, especially the last sentence. There is another change here. What are the possible meanings of those last two and a half lines?

 Learning checkpoint

As in many poems, the last lines call for special attention: 'But today / It is my father who keeps stumbling / Behind me, and will not go away.'

The writer has deliberately ended the poem with a surprising and puzzling statement.

Discuss what you think this statement means with a partner. There are a number of possible interpretations and you should not worry that the meaning is ambiguous. Writers, especially poets, often like to leave some things open to the reader's interpretation. When you write about aspects of a text that you find puzzling, don't be afraid to say so – as long as you can set out reasons for your thoughts and ideas.

GETTING IT INTO WRITING

1 Using the work you have already done, together with further ideas you have had while considering the contrasts and the ending, write a paragraph or two to answer the question: **How does the poem show Heaney's feelings about his father?**

2 Here are two example responses. Compare them with your own and discuss how well they each answer the question.

As a boy, Seamus Heaney looked up to his father and wanted to be like him and to do the things that he did, especially to manage the horse and plough so expertly. His father was very strong and capable but Seamus was small and probably a distraction to his father as he tried to work. But his father put up with him and carried him on his back. Nowadays, his father is old and infirm and Seamus has to look after him, which is the other way around. He resents this a bit because he says he will not go away.

Heaney clearly admires his father for his skill with the plough and the horses. He spends time describing in detail (the click of his tongue, the single pluck of the reins) the ways his father showed that he was 'An expert'. Looking back, he describes himself in negative terms, tripping, falling and 'a nuisance'. He felt that he was in his father's shadow, literally and figuratively, and though he wanted to follow in his father's footsteps, obviously he did not. However, now that he is grown up, his father is the one who stumbles and needs to be looked after. We do not know if it is the memory of his father that will not go away or if he feels some irritation that he is still around.

Comparing poems

1 Both Heaney's 'Follower' and Day-Lewis's 'Walking Away' use metaphor and simile to help the reader to envisage what they have seen or to convey some of the feelings that they have. Compare the use of comparisons (whether metaphor or simile) in the two poems using these starting points as a guide:

Heaney uses the image of a sailor in order to …

He returns to this image later in the poem, for example …

Day-Lewis uses several different images to convey the idea of …

In my opinion, the most effective of these is …

Both poems employ simile and metaphor but I prefer … because …

2 A poet's **diction** is their choice of words, such as particular nouns and adjectives, rather than images. How do 'Follower' and 'Walking Away' compare when you look at this aspect of language?

Your response

1 What do you feel is the overall tone of the poem? Here are some suggestions:

nostalgia   regret   admiration   resignation   sadness

2 In what ways could Heaney's thoughts be applied to people you know?

His shoulders globed like a full sail strung

GETTING CREATIVE

This is another writer's 'version' of Heaney's poem. Read it and then try writing your own version of 'Follower' – it could be about a family member or another adult you knew when you were younger.

My father worked with a fork and spade
His hands rough with the pulling of weeds
And the management of handle and blade.
The shed bench littered with packets of seeds.

An expert. He would set the seedlings
In neat rows labelled with Latin names:
Rows made straight with sticks and string.
In the greenhouse, in the cold frame,

His eye narrowed and angled on aphid
Or wasp. He'd use knife, fingers or
Pungent poisonous fumes to rid
The greenhouse of pests. I saw

A navy blue apron with pockets for plants,
Secateurs, garden knife, bits of bass
To tie up the dahlias, tomatoes, chrysanths;
I'd 'help' if I could with each task.

'Don't be a gardener, son,' he'd say
Not for the work, but the pay.
And was glad when books took me away
And gave me things he'd never had.

Love and relationships
11 Mother, any distance

GETTING STARTED – THE POEM AND YOU

1 Look at the title of the poem. Why do you think Armitage addresses the poem to 'Mother' rather than 'Mum'? Might it be because:

a   his mother doesn't like being called 'Mum'
b   it's more formal
c   it makes the poem read like a letter
d   he doesn't think of her as 'Mum'?

Can you think of any other reason?

2 This poem reflects on leaving home and putting a distance between yourself and your parents. In pairs, discuss:

a   three advantages of leaving home
b   three disadvantages of leaving home.

GETTING CLOSER – FOCUS ON DETAILS

First impressions

1 After a quick first reading of 'Mother, any distance', list the five words that you think are most important in the poem.

2 How would you use these five words in one or two sentences to introduce the poem to someone who has not yet read it?

3 Which of these phrases do you think best describes the movement through the poem:

a   from dependence to independence
b   from present to future
c   from being close to being apart
d   from security to risk?

 Contexts

Simon Armitage was born in Huddersfield in 1963.

This poem is taken from *Book of Matches*, a collection of 30 sonnets which Armitage wrote for his 30th birthday. The sonnets are based on a party game in which the players talk about their lives in the time it takes for a match to burn (around 20 seconds). In the original book, none of the poems

have titles, but they all start with an asterisk, which represents somebody striking a match.

Can you read this poem in 20 seconds?

You can read a prose account of Armitage's childhood in *Little Green Man* and his other prose work *All Points North*.

MOTHER, ANY DISTANCE

Mother, any distance greater than a single span
requires a second pair of hands.
You come to help me measure windows, pelmets, doors,
the acres of the walls, the prairies of the floors.

You at the zero-end, me with the spool of tape, recording
length, reporting metres, centimetres back to base, then leaving   5
up the stairs, the line still feeding out, unreeling
years between us. Anchor. Kite.

I space-walk through the empty bedrooms, climb
the ladder to the loft, to breaking point, where something has to give;
two floors below your fingertips still pinch   10
the last one-hundredth of an inch … I reach
towards a hatch that opens on an endless sky
to fall or fly.

Simon Armitage

pelmet (3): panel used
to cover the top part of
curtains

prairies (4): uninhabited
area of open, treeless
grassland in America

 Listen to the poem on Cambridge Elevate

Interpreting themes, ideas, attitudes and feelings

1 Working in pairs, explore these statements about the poem and add any of your own. Put them in order to show how far you agree with them. Add a detail from the poem that supports each statement.

Statement	Supporting detail from the poem
He is putting more and more distance between them.	
He is describing how it feels to get away from his mother.	
He is enjoying his freedom.	
He wonders if he is able to break free.	
He resents his mother's presence.	
He is aware that there are strong ties between them.	
He is grateful for his mother's help.	

2 Rewrite the poem as if written by the mother. It will only need a small number of changes. For example start by changing the word 'Mother' in the first line to 'Son'.

3 Write two or three sentences about the changes that made the most difference. How well does your version present the mother's feelings about her son leaving home?

I space-walk through the
empty bedrooms

PUTTING DETAILS TO USE

Analysing language, form and structure

1 List the verbs in the poem, especially those describing actions.

2 How would you act out the poem? In groups, one person could act out the poem while the others call out the verbs as they see them.

Armitage makes the poem more interesting by using the situation of measuring in a new home to reveal something about the feelings and ideas that spring from close relationships. This is where the reader interprets what the writer thinks and feels.

3 The poet describes his mother as an 'anchor'. Explore some of the ideas and connections with ships by answering these questions:

  a   What does an anchor do?
  b   Where, usually, do ships anchor?
  c   Why is an anchor necessary?
  d   What happens if a ship loses its anchor?

4 Armitage describes himself as a 'kite'. Some of the possible connections are:

  - a kite is built to fly high
  - a kite is controlled by the person flying it
  - a kite has no power of its own.

Can you think of any others? What happens if the kite-line breaks?

5 What do you think Armitage means at the end of the poem where he wonders whether he may 'fall' or 'fly'?

Learning checkpoint

Write a couple of paragraphs in response to your exploration of the poem so far. Show how you are building on understanding to develop your own interpretation of the poem, and how you are exploring the poem to make use of implied meanings.

PSI (poetry scene investigation)

1 In a previous activity you explored the use of verbs in the poem. Now explore the nouns and noun phrases, for example 'pair of hands' or 'spool of tape'.

Sort your collection into categories. You could use these headings as a starting place, or decide your own.

Distance	Measurement
Connection	Tethering

2 Look at Armitage's word choice in:

two floors below your <u>fingertips</u> still <u>pinch</u>

To analyse his choice of words, start by thinking of other words he could have used, but didn't.

  a   He could have used 'hand' or 'finger'. Why do you think he chose 'finger<u>tips</u>' instead?
  b   He could have used a word such as 'hold', 'grasp' or 'grip' to convey his mother's action. Why do you think he chose 'pinch' instead?

3 Explore three other noun choices in this way. What do they tell you about the poet's feelings?

4 Look at Armitage's use of **syntax**. Verse two has one long sentence running over three and a half lines, followed by two words standing as a sentence each. What effect do you think he wanted by writing the two words this way?

Learning checkpoint

Choose five words or phrases from the poem and explain why you think Armitage selected each of them. Be willing to add queries or possibilities of your own. Link your explanations to the theme of the poem. Finish with a sentence or two that sums up what you have discovered. You may wish to use this as a starting point:

'unreeling'	He is getting further away from her but is still connected. A fishing line unreels but is not always connected to anything (and has a hook on the end). The idea of a kite line is better as the connection remains, even though the kite gets further away (and being higher is seen as a good thing).
'endless sky'	
'breaking point'	
'prairies'	
'a second pair of hands'	

Show your skills

Look at the following examples of writing about the poem. Notice where the writer has started to explore the poem more deeply and offers possible interpretations and opinions. How far do you agree with what has been written?

He may mean that he can't get away because he is tied to her like a ship. Or it may mean he is safe because without an anchor he might drift off and hit the rocks. An anchor can be a restraint or a security. From the rest of the poem, I think he means security.

He uses the word 'fingertips' rather than 'fingers' or 'hand' because the fingertips are the very end of the hand. His mother is only just in touch with him. 'Fingertips' also reminds us of 'hanging on by your fingertips', which suggests something quite desperate, which may be how one of them is feeling.

The poem gives us Armitage's viewpoint as the son. We can imagine the mother's viewpoint from her movements 'reeling' and 'pinching', accepting that she has to let her son go, but hoping that she can keep some contact – if not control – over him. The parent's perspective is not explicit in the poem but some readers would see it.

GETTING IT INTO WRITING

Using the work you have already done in the Learning checkpoints as a starting point, sum up what you know about the poem and what your interpretations are. You may wish to use these phrases as guides:

The poem describes Armitage and his mother measuring …

As the poem goes on, you realise that …

He uses the image of … to …

He also refers to … which makes the reader think of …

Armitage shows through his use of … that he feels …

His mother's feelings are less clear, but …

I think that the poem shows …

Comparing poems

Compare this poem with another that presents family relationships, for example 'Follower' (son's view of father) or 'Walking Away' (father's view of son). You might also want to look ahead to the next unit, in which the poem 'Before You Were Mine' presents a daughter's view of her mother.

When making your comparison, you might want to think about:

- ideas, perspectives and contexts
- language, form and structure – and how the writer uses these to affect the reader
- your own opinions about the poems.

Another option would be to explore an 'unseen' poem about family relationships by another **contemporary** writer, for example Gillian Clarke's 'Catrin' or Vernon Scannell's 'Nettles'.

Your response

1 Imagine that you are the poet's mother. What might your feelings be on reading it for the first time?

2 Overall, do you feel that Armitage was keen or reluctant to become independent – or did he have mixed feelings?

Explore the poem further with a storyboard activity on Cambridge Elevate

to breaking point, where something has to give

12 Before You Were Mine

GETTING STARTED – THE POEM AND YOU

1 What do you think your parents/carers were like before you were around? How would you find out?

2 Read 'Before You Were Mine'. Duffy seems to know a lot of very specific detail about her mother. How might she know it? Could some of it be imagined?

GETTING CLOSER – FOCUS ON DETAILS

First impressions

What kind of a person do you think Duffy's mother was? Arrange these adjectives in a diamond shape (1-2-3-2-1) with the most appropriate at the top and the least at the bottom:

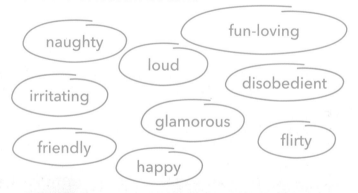

naughty
fun-loving
loud
disobedient
irritating
glamorous
flirty
friendly
happy

> **ℹ Contexts**
>
> This poem is by Carol Ann Duffy – the first woman (and the first person from Scotland) to be British Poet Laureate, which she has been since 2009.

Interpreting themes, ideas, attitudes and feelings

1 One way to get close to a poem is to put your own words inside it. Try rewriting the first verse of the poem without the line endings so that it reads as a prose description. Insert your own words as necessary in order to make the meaning clearer for you. For example it may help you to know that the poet's mother is called Marilyn but the end of the first verse is also a reference to a famous picture of the film star Marilyn Monroe.

2 Now do the same with the other verses. (Hint: If you find this difficult, look ahead to the questions and pointers in 'Putting details to use'.)

> **✔ Learning checkpoint**
>
> What do you now know about the writer's mother? What can you infer? What do you know about the writer as a child? What can you infer?
>
> You could organise your findings as a diagram. Put the things you are most certain of near the centre of the diagram and those that are an educated guess further out.
>
> Compare your diagram with a partner and then with as wide a group as possible. It may be feasible to create a large class diagram. At each stage, be prepared to explain why you have added a finding and your level of certainty. Be ready to question other students' findings, too.

Listen to the poem on Cambridge Elevate

BEFORE YOU WERE MINE

I'm ten years away from the corner you laugh on
with your pals, Maggie McGeeney and Jean Duff.
The three of you bend from the waist, holding
each other, or your knees, and shriek at the pavement.
Your polka-dot dress blows round your legs. Marilyn.   5

I'm not here yet. The thought of me doesn't occur
in the ballroom with the thousand eyes, the fizzy, movie tomorrows
the right walk home could bring. I knew you would dance
like that. Before you were mine, your Ma stands at the close
with a hiding for the late one. You reckon it's worth it.   10

The decade ahead of my loud, possessive yell was the best one, eh?
I remember my hands in those high-heeled red shoes, relics,
and now your ghost clatters toward me over George Square
till I see you, clear as scent, under the tree,
with its lights, and whose small bites on your neck, sweetheart?   15

Cha cha cha! You'd teach me the steps on the way home from Mass,
stamping stars from the wrong pavement. Even then
I wanted the bold girl winking in Portobello, somewhere
in Scotland, before I was born. That glamorous love lasts
where you sparkle and waltz and laugh before you were mine.   20

Carol Ann Duffy

PUTTING DETAILS TO USE

As you work through the poem, you may find you have some questions. Here is an example of verses two to four with some pointers to guide you.

I'm not here yet. The thought of me doesn't occur
in the ballroom with the thousand eyes, the fizzy, movie tomorrows
the right walk home could bring. I knew you would dance
like that. Before you were mine, your Ma stands at the close
with a hiding for the late one. You reckon it's worth it.

Search images of 'glitterball', 'disco ball' or 'mirror ball'

Romantic ideas from films?

What might be 'right' about it?

(noun) What kind of road?

The decade ahead of my loud, possessive yell was the best one, eh?
I remember my hands in those high-heeled red shoes, relics,
and now your ghost clatters toward me over George Square
till I see you, clear as scent, under the tree,
with its lights, and whose small bites on your neck, sweetheart?

Can have several meanings – which ones might be intended here?

A memory or an imagined person – which?

Can smells bring back memories?

Who is imagined as saying this?

Cha cha cha! You'd teach me the steps on the way home from Mass,
stamping stars from the wrong pavement. Even then
I wanted the bold girl winking in Portobello, somewhere
in Scotland, before I was born. That glamorous love lasts
where you sparkle and waltz and laugh before you were mine.

What were the 'steps'?

What does this tell you about the family?

Why is this now the 'wrong' pavement?

This is vague – why?

GETTING IT INTO WRITING

1 You now have enough material to write about the poet's mother both before Carol Ann Duffy was born and afterwards. Use what you have learned to write a character description of about 200 words.

2 Now think about how the writer feels about her mother and how she views all the memories and stories she has heard. This will depend on **your** interpretation of the poem but will still need to be based on evidence from the text. You could do this by thinking aloud as if you were the daughter:

> 'I loved hearing about how she went out dancing as a teenager. I can imagine her being the lively chatty girl who flirted with all the boys in the dance hall …'

3 Turn those thoughts into a paragraph describing the poet's feelings about her mother and what the relationship between them was like.

Show your skills

Exchange your piece of writing with a partner. Read through and make short notes in the margin with a pencil to show where you have noticed that your partner has:

A described the poet's feelings about her mother and referred to the text

B inferred something from the text about the relationship

C offered some thoughts about the relationship, which can be justified from the text but are not explicitly stated there.

For example:

Partner's writing	Your notes
The two of them had a happy relationship – for example, she taught her dance steps …	B
Carol Ann Duffy likes the image of her mother as a teenager enjoying herself ('I wanted the bold girl …')	A
It is as if she envies her mother's lifestyle as it was then and is perhaps wistful that having a child has put an end to all that youthful enjoyment.	C

You will then need to look at your own description and see how well you did. Hopefully you will have a number of As and Bs but also some Cs, which will show you are writing with a high level of analysis.

Comparing poems

The poem deals with the viewpoint of the writer in an unusual way. There is the standpoint of the grown-up writer who imagines a time before she was born and then recreates a time when, as a young girl, she was already thinking of her mother's past.

When you read other poems, think about where the writer is standing in time and place and whether it varies. Look back at 'Follower' and 'Eden Rock' and notice how the viewpoint of the writer alters in each poem.

Your response

How would you describe the overall feel or tone of the poem? Where can you detect quieter notes? Here are some suggestions to which you can add your own.

exuberant	frantic	carefree	lively
reflective	jolly	energetic	wistful
nostalgic	sad	humorous	loving

 Explore the poem further with a video activity on Cambridge Elevate

Love and relationships
13 Winter Swans

GETTING STARTED – THE POEM AND YOU

1. What associations do swans have for you? In no more than a minute, jot down all the things that come to mind without thinking too much about them.

2. Compare and share your list with that of a partner. Combine your ideas and divide them into two categories: physical (description) and abstract (ideas). Physical qualities would include things like 'long neck' or actions such as 'gliding on the water'. Abstract qualities would include concepts such as 'purity'.

3. Combine your list with that of another pair. Are there any surprises? Are there any negative qualities?

4. Now read 'Winter Swans'.

   Which of the qualities on your combined list are reflected in the poem?

GETTING CLOSER – FOCUS ON DETAILS

First impressions

1. Without looking back at the poem, write down four things you remember about the swans as described by Sheers.

2. Write a paragraph beginning, *Owen Sheers describes the swans as being …* Include the four things you remembered as part of your paragraph.

Interpreting themes, ideas, attitudes and feelings

The writer is using the image of the swans to signify something more than the fact that they saw some nice birds in the park. What do you think the birds symbolise for him? Love/affection/togetherness/romance/long-lasting relationships or something else? Do you think that they are an appropriate symbol? What other symbols could be used?

 Contexts

Owen Sheers (born in 1974) is a Welsh writer and poet. Welsh history and identity is an important theme in his writing. As well as poetry, he also writes fiction, non-fiction and drama. His novel *Resistance* has been turned into a film.

Sheers is writer-in-residence at the Welsh Rugby Union, having been a rugby player himself. You may have seen one of his regular appearances as a presenter on TV. This poem is from his collection called *Skirrid Hill*.

WINTER SWANS

The clouds had given their all —
two days of rain and then a break
in which we walked,

the waterlogged earth
gulping for breath at our feet   5
as we skirted the lake, silent and apart,

until the swans came and stopped us
with a show of tipping in unison.
As if rolling weights down their bodies to their heads

they halved themselves in the dark water,   10
icebergs of white feather, paused before returning again
like boats righting in rough weather.

'They mate for life' you said as they left,
porcelain over the stilling water. I didn't reply
but as we moved on through the afternoon light,   15

slow-stepping in the lake's shingle and sand,
I noticed our hands, that had, somehow,
swum the distance between us

and folded, one over the other,
like a pair of wings settling after flight.   20

Owen Sheers

 Listen to the poem on Cambridge Elevate

PUTTING DETAILS TO USE

Analysing language, form and structure

1 This is a poem that could be seen as prose. It's not very long – only four sentences – so write it out without the line breaks and read it through again.

2 You may notice that, apart from the third one, the sentences are rather complex. The number of sub-clauses and phrases means that reading them can be quite difficult. The last sentence stretches over three verses, from line 14 to line 20.

Can you work out where the main clause, the central action, of this last sentence is?

There is a lot of action in that main clause (or to be precise, clauses). He **noticed**, hands **swum**, hands **folded** as well as a non-action: did **not reply**. If we include the rest of the sentence, we have 'moved', 'slow-stepping', and, 'settling'. That's a lot going on in a short space. Look back at the first two sentences and see if there is as much happening in those.

What appears to be a very peaceful little description, a snapshot or short video of a romantic moment, has been created through a lot of hard work. Under the surface, those sentences are paddling very hard!

Show your skills

Make a checklist to show what you have learned so far. Make two columns, one for things you definitely know and one for things that you are fairly sure of. The second column may be things you have inferred or 'read between the lines' and may be phrased as questions.

For example:

What I know	What I wonder...
This is a poem about two people walking by a lake after heavy rain.	Have they had an argument or are they just in their own worlds?
The poem does not rhyme or have a particular pattern.	
	The swans symbolise ...

I noticed our hands, that had, somehow, swum the distance between us

and folded, one over the other, like a pair of wings settling after flight.

Learning checkpoint

One of the following responses to the above task is better than the other – but in what ways?

A I like 'icebergs of white feather' because icebergs are white and float on the water just like the swans – and it is very simple and easy to understand.

B 'Icebergs of white feather' is effective because icebergs are also seen on cold water and their colour will be similar. Perhaps also there is a lot of the iceberg beneath the water and we know that the swans' legs and feet will be paddling under the water, unseen. Also, icebergs seem peaceful but are in fact dangerous as swans can be.

GETTING IT INTO WRITING

1 Look at the use of imagery in 'Winter Swans', which works on more than one level. There are descriptions of the swans themselves and their movements and then there is the image of hands reflecting the movement of swans' wings. The latter image goes further because the hands themselves represent more than fingery appendages.

Write a paragraph focusing on the use of imagery regarding the swans (you may or may not wish to distinguish between simile and metaphor). Remember to use evidence from the poem to back up what you say.

2 Write 200–300 words in answer to the question: **How do we know the swans are so important to the poet in recollecting the experience of walking by the lake?** Start by making a bullet-point list of all the reasons why the swans seem to fit with Sheers' experience and his mood. Your list might include:

- rainy day cheered up by swans
- sight of swans made them stop, changed their day
- fascinated by their actions and their appearance
- shows careful observation of swans
- describes them in different, positive ways.

Your essay might begin in one of the following ways:

The swans are particularly important to the writer because they coincided with an experience that …

The day started off dreary and he and his partner had been walking silently and apart until …

The swans made a big difference to the writer …

Sheers remembers the swans very fondly because …

Comparing poems

This poem is interesting for what it **doesn't** say. It sketches the situation and allows readers to fill in the details. In this way it is very different to 'Singh Song!', which is covered in the next unit. How does it compare to any other love poem you've read? You can find a varied selection in the 'love poems' section of the Poetry Foundation website.

 Read love poems from the Poetry Foundation website on Cambridge Elevate

Your response

If something like this happened to you, would you write about it or keep it to yourself? How do you think the other person feels about being a character in a poem?

Love and relationships
14 Singh Song!

GETTING STARTED – THE POEM AND YOU

1 What do you expect from a poem titled 'Singh Song!'? (What does sing-song mean?) Could it actually be a song sung by someone called Singh?

From the beginning, we suspect that the writer is playing with language – and maybe also playing with our expectations.

2 Read only the first verse:

I run just one ov my daddy's shops
from 9 o'clock to 9 o'clock
and he vunt me not to hav a break
but ven nobody in, I do di lock —

Are your expectations confirmed or changed?

GETTING CLOSER – FOCUS ON DETAILS

First impressions

1 In a group or as a class, read it aloud, taking turns with different lines. Don't worry if you don't understand all of it to begin with.

2 With a partner, discuss the following questions:

a What do you think are the main themes of the poem?
b Why do you think the poet wrote the poem?

SINGH SONG!

I run just one ov my daddy's shops
from 9 o'clock to 9 o'clock
and he vunt me not to hav a break
but ven nobody in, I do di lock —

cos up di stairs is my newly bride 5
vee share in chapatti
vee share in di chutney
after vee hav made luv
like vee rowing through Putney —

Ven I return vid my pinnie untied 10
di shoppers always point and cry:
Hey Singh, ver yoo bin?
Yor lemons are limes
yor bananas are plantain,
dis dirty little floor need a little bit of mop 15
in di worst Indian shop
on di whole Indian road —

Above my head high heel tap di ground
as my vife on di web is playing wid di mouse
ven she netting two cat on her Sikh lover site   20
she book dem for di meat at di cheese ov her
   price —

my bride
     she effing at my mum
     in all di colours of Punjabi
     den stumble like a drunk   25
     making fun at my daddy

my bride
     tiny eyes ov a gun
     and di tummy ov a teddy

my bride   30
     she hav a red crew cut
     and she wear a Tartan sari
     a donkey jacket and some pumps
     on di squeak ov di girls dat are pinching
       my sweeties —

Ven I return from di tickle ov my bride   35
di shoppers always point and cry:
Hey Singh, ver yoo bin?
Di milk is out ov date
and di bread is alvays stale,
di tings yoo hav on offer yoo hav never got in
   stock   40
in di worst Indian shop
on di whole Indian road —

Late in di midnight hour
ven yoo shoppers are wrap up quiet
ven di precinct is concrete-cool   45
vee cum down whispering stairs
and sit on my silver stool,
from behind di chocolate bars
vee stare past di half-price window signs
at di beaches ov di UK in di brightey moon —   50

from di stool each night she say,
     How much do yoo charge for dat moon baby?

from di stool each night I say,
     Is half di cost ov yoo baby,

from di stool each night she say,   55
     How much does dat come to baby?

from di stool each night I say,
     Is priceless baby —

Daljit Nagra

pinnie (10): apron
plantain (14): a green fruit
of the banana family

🔊 Listen to the poem on Cambridge Elevate

Interpreting themes, ideas, attitudes and feelings

'Singh Song!' addresses a number of stereotypes. It takes certain expectations about Indian shopkeepers and undermines them. Complete these statements, using the first one as an example:

a   Indian shopkeepers are expected to be open all hours but … *this shopkeeper closes when he can.*

b   Indian shopkeepers are expected to be hard-working but …

c   You would expect Mr Singh to respect his father but …

d   You would expect his wife to …

Learning checkpoint

Write a few sentences about how the poet deals with stereotypes, using brief quotes from the poem to illustrate your points.

Contexts

Daljit Nagra is a British poet born in 1966 to Sikh Punjabi parents who came to Britain from India in the late 1950s. He grew up near Heathrow Airport in West London. He was 19 when he first started reading poetry, and it was the poems of William Blake (see Cluster 2 Unit 2) that inspired him to study English Literature and become a poet.

His poetry explores the experience of 'first generation' immigrants to Britain. This poem and its use of English pokes fun at his own culture and at Indian stereotypes. You can find video clips online of Daljit Nagra speaking this poem. He encourages readers to speak the poem aloud in an Indian accent. Try it!

PUTTING DETAILS TO USE

Analysing language, form and structure

1   What kind of poem do you think this is?

You will need to do some research to find out what some of these terms mean. Then work with a partner to list these descriptions in order, with the most appropriate description at the top and the least appropriate at the bottom. You may wish to give some of the terms equal status.

chant   song   performance poem   love poem   praise song   dramatic monologue   satire   narrative poem   rap

2 As a class, discuss the most popular descriptions and how well the text fits those categories. It isn't necessary to be able to pigeonhole every poem, but it is useful to have some knowledge of the kinds of terms that are used to describe various kinds of writing.

3 Replace the 'Punglish' spellings with **standard English** in one of the verses. For example, change 'di' to 'the', 'ven' to 'when' and so on, and insert any words you feel are 'missing' from a standard English version.

4 Now read your standard English version aloud. How does the rewriting affect your reading of the poem?

Some poems are meant to be spoken or performed. A rap written out in standard English looks a bit ridiculous. Other poems are printed in a particular way (for example with gaps between verses that would not be noticed by a listener) to be seen on the page. Look out for these differences as you encounter other poems or look back at the ones you have already read.

Show your skills

How far does this example show that the writer is moving from explaining towards exploring the text?

Many people would expect an Indian shopkeeper to be very hard-working and anxious to make a success of the business. However, Singh is not concerned with keeping his shop open. He will 'do di lock' as soon as he can and spend time with his 'newly bride'. Nor does he keep it clean and well stocked, as his customers complain that the milk is out of date and the bread is stale. The fact that he sings about these things and is proud to spend time with his wife with her red crew cut shows he really doesn't care about worldly things. That becomes even clearer when we hear that they spend time looking at the moon, which is 'priceless, baby'.

from di stool each night she say,
How much do yoo charge for dat moon baby?

GETTING IT INTO WRITING

1 Write two or three sentences to explain to someone who has not seen or heard 'Singh Song!' what kind of a poem it is and how it is different from other poems – especially other love poems – they may have come across.

2 Here are some examples of students' free writing about 'Singh Song!'. Pick out the phrases in these statements that you think are true. Make a note of any aspects you think have been missed.

'Singh Song!' is a strange poem because it's not really a song you could sing, it's more of a happy kind of chant that the writer has put together just for the fun of it.

He wants to show off that he has a new bride who is a bit of a rebel or a bit unusual but he really loves her and enjoys singing about him and her.

He doesn't really care about the shop, which is a shame because customers will stop coming and then he and his wife won't be so happy.

The verses of 'Singh Song!' are all over the place. Some parts rhyme and others don't. I suppose it might all fit together if there was some music to go with it.

The writer is having a laugh at the shopkeeper – but not in a nasty way. He kind of likes and admires him.

3 Now, using those points, together with further thoughts of your own, create a few paragraphs (total 100–200 words) exploring what you think of the poem and what you think Nagra is trying to convey. One important question for you to answer by the end of your piece of writing is: **How far does the poet succeed in what you think he sets out to do?**

Comparing poems

Which poem from this cluster will you choose to compare with 'Singh Song!'? Although the form and style of Elizabeth Barrett Browning's 'I think of thee!' are very different from Nagra's poem, the sonnet might make a good comparison as both poems describe genuine love between husbands and wives. Another option might be 'Before You Were Mine', as both poems contain 'everyday' language and humour. Do you think that any of the other poems in the cluster challenge preconceived ideas, in the way that Nagra uses his poem to challenge stereotypes?

Whichever poem you choose, start by making a list of similarities and differences between the two poems.

Your response

How does 'Singh Song!' compare with love songs you have heard? Can you think of any that have as much detail about the object of the singer's affection? How many mention wives or husbands?

my bride
she hav a red crew cut
and she wear a Tartan sari

Love and relationships
15 Climbing My Grandfather

GETTING STARTED – THE POEM AND YOU

This poem is a description with a difference! Read it and then answer the following questions:

a   How carefully could you describe a person such as a grandparent from memory? (For example do you even know the colour of their eyes?)

b   Think about an older person you know and jot down everything about their appearance that you can remember. Make a note of all the things you cannot remember.

GETTING CLOSER – FOCUS ON DETAILS

First impressions

Getting closer is exactly what this poem does. This amount of detail about a person would probably become tedious if expressed as a simple description. Waterhouse's unusual approach enables him to describe his grandfather in great detail in a way that is not just interesting but intriguing.

Read the poem through again and then put yourself in the position of the larger person and imagine someone small climbing up you. Write about what you notice as they ascend your body. To help you do this, you could think about the following questions:

a   When do you first notice them?

b   Is it touch, sight or maybe sound you notice first?

c   What difficulties do they encounter?

d   What details would they notice along the way?

Interpreting themes, ideas, attitudes and feelings

Which of these statements do you think describes the writer's feelings about his grandfather? You can adapt or write your own statement if none of these seem to fit:

a   He admires his grandfather for his continuing strength.

b   He loves his grandfather but would like to feel closer to him.

c   He respects his grandfather for carrying on working physically.

d   He is concerned about his grandfather's health and age.

 Contexts

Andrew Waterhouse (1958–2001) grew up in the north-east of England. He was a poet and musician, and was very passionate about the environment. After winning a prestigious poetry prize in 2000, he gave up his job teaching to devote his time to writing. He was a very private person, who struggled with depression, and the following year he took his own life. This memorable poem is a portrait of his grandfather, but from a very unusual perspective.

CLIMBING MY GRANDFATHER

I decide to do it free, without a rope or net.
First, the old brogues, dusty and cracked;
an easy scramble onto his trousers,
pushing into the weave, trying to get a grip.
By the overhanging shirt I change   5
direction, traverse along his belt
to an earth stained hand. The nails
are splintered and give good purchase,
The skin of his finger is smooth and thick
like warm ice. On his arm I discover   10
the glassy ridge of a scar, place my feet
gently in the old stitches and move on.
At his still firm shoulder, I rest for a while
in the shade, not looking down,
for climbing has its dangers, then pull   15
myself up the loose skin of his neck
to a smiling mouth to drink among teeth.
Refreshed, I cross the screed cheek,
to stare into his brown eyes, watch a pupil
slowly open and close. Then up over   20
the forehead, the wrinkles well-spaced
and easy, to his thick hair (soft and white
at this altitude), reaching for the summit,
where gasping for breath I can only lie
watching clouds and birds circle,   25
feeling his heat, knowing
the slow pulse of his good heart.

Andrew Waterhouse

◀)) Listen to the poem on Cambridge Elevate

PUTTING DETAILS TO USE

1 Annotate a copy of the poem to highlight the words and phrases that link the description to the idea of a climb. Now underline or circle the details of the grandfather's appearance. Notice how the two aspects are interwoven and sometimes overlap. For example:

> On his arm I discover
>
> the glassy <u>ridge of a scar</u>, place my feet
>
> gently in the <u>old stitches</u> and move on.

2 This poem could be seen as an example of an extended metaphor. Why do you think the writer is describing his grandfather as though he were a mountain? Write a sentence describing what mountains and mountain climbing make you think of.

Analysing language, form and structure

1 Write the poem out as prose. Without looking back at the original, where would you insert line breaks in the text? Compare your decisions with those of the poet. Are they the same? Perhaps yours are better?

2 Once again, highlight a copy of the poem, this time to mark the writer's use of nouns, adjectives and verbs.

You might expect there to be more verbs, as this is a piece of writing about movement and action. The strength of the poem seems to lie more in the nouns. They, like the adjectives, tend to be short (one or two syllables) words in everyday use. In other words, there is little about the language choices of the writer that you could call 'poetic' – but extended metaphors are a common feature of poetry.

Show your skills

The poem provides a detailed description of the physical appearance of the writer's grandfather, but it also hints at the older man's character and the feelings of the grandson towards him. What else does the poem tell us about the two characters?

Look closely at these examples of students' writing. Think about whether they just explain or go further and explore. Do they deal with what is implicit or stick with what is explicit?

We can tell that the writer's grandfather is a nice old man because it says that he is smiling and at the end we are told he has a 'good heart', which does not just mean he is healthy. I think the grandfather has had a hard life because he has scars and his hands are earth stained. The writer loves his grandfather and shows it in the way he writes so carefully. He would not write in such detail if he did not care deeply.

 Learning checkpoint

What do you think of the way the description of the grandfather is written? When you see a poem that looks like it would make more sense written out as prose, a good thing to ask yourself is: **Why**? Why do you think the writer has chosen to use the form of a poem? Try to think of points in favour of it and against it. For example:

For	Against
The unusual idea of the climb up someone's body is more suitable for poetry because …	The writer's description of his grandfather doesn't need to be a poem because …
The poet has chosen specific places to break the lines to have an effect on the reader. For example …	

The grandfather seems to be a hard-working man, engaged in physical labour. He is still active, still wearing his dusty old brogues and having earth-stained hands and splintered nails. His hands are solid and though the skin on his neck is loose, the shoulder is still firm. This gives an impression of strength and endurance. In spite of a life of toil, he has come through accidents (the ridge of a scar) and probably other misfortunes and is now having a moment of rest. The last lines say more about the writer than the grandfather. He believes the old man is 'good-hearted' and he sees the smiling mouth. Throughout the poem there is nothing negative at all – even the splintered nails have a positive purpose!

GETTING IT INTO WRITING

Comparing poems

You will now have read several poems about the relationships between children and parents or grandparents. This writing task asks you to compare two poems, 'Climbing My Grandfather' and 'Follower'. Read through 'Follower' again and then think how the two poems are similar and in what ways they differ. You may find a table useful in order to organise your ideas. For example:

'Climbing My Grandfather'	'Follower'
Both of the poems are about …	
The poem is written in **free verse**, which …	The poem has a definite pattern, which …
It uses an unusual comparison in order to …	
The vocabulary used …	
	The poet states his feelings clearly. He feels that …
	There are many contrasts in the poem. For example …
Also, I noticed that …	
To me, the most important thing about the poem is …	
Although the two poems have a lot in common …	

Your response

Is this a good way to describe a person – or does it concentrate too much on appearances and say too little about a person's character?

traverse along his belt
to an earth stained hand. The nails
are splintered and give good purchase

Love and relationships
16 Comparing poems

What you have to do

If you are studying Cluster 1 'Love and relationships' from the anthology, then in Section B of your poetry exam you will need to compare two poems from this cluster.

- One poem from Cluster 1 will be printed for you on the exam paper.
- Once you know the question, you will need to choose another poem from Cluster 1 to compare the named poem with.
- You will not have your anthology with you in the exam room.
- You will have around 45 minutes to write your comparison.

The comparison question

The question you are asked in the exam will give you a focus for your comparison. For example:

> Compare how poets present attitudes towards a parent in 'Follower' and in **one** other poem from 'Love and relationships'.
>
> **[30 marks]**

Read the question carefully and focus your comparison on what the question asks. The focus in this question is on the underlined words and phrases.

The focus of the question might vary depending on the poem. For example you might be asked about the **attitudes** or **ideas** in the poem, and the focus might be on love relationships, relationships between parents and children, or another aspect of the poem.

Until you see the poem and the question, you will not know the focus of your comparison. However, your study of the poems in your GCSE course should mean that you know each poem in the cluster so well that you will feel prepared and confident. Show your skills by choosing a poem to compare that gives you lots to say in response to the focus of the question.

Comparing poems

Comparing poems simply means writing about **similarities** and **differences** in the **content** and **style** of two poems.

The most obvious similarity is that the two poems from Cluster 1 will be about love and relationships. The similarities and differences that matter are **what** the poets have to say about love and relationships (content), and **how** they say it (style).

The **content** is what's in the poem. Depending on the poem, this might include:

- situations, experiences, people, places
- ideas, thoughts, feelings, attitudes, perspectives, contexts
- setting, atmosphere.

The **style** is how the poem is written. You will write about the poem's style in relation to its content, and analyse the choices the poet has made to express their ideas. This might include:

- use of language – tone and techniques
- structure
- form, and the pattern of rhythm and rhyme.

Similarities and differences

Comparing two poems can help you to understand each poem more clearly, as you often notice different things when you explore poems side by side. It's similar in some ways to when you buy a new mobile phone or some new trainers and look at a variety of features side by side to make the best choice.

When you are thinking about comparison, let the poems speak for themselves. Students sometimes tie themselves in knots inventing similarities that cannot easily be supported by evidence from the texts.

It can be more productive to think about differences than similarities, though you are encouraged to do both. If you think about style as being something individual (in the same way as that styles of dress and styles of architecture can be individual, for instance), it is likely that you will find more differences than similarities in style in poetry, too.

How you will be assessed

The Assessment Objectives (AOs) outline the skills you need to demonstrate in order to be successful. In the anthology question the three AOs are:

AO1: Read, understand and respond to texts. Students should be able to:

- maintain a critical style and develop an informed personal response
- use textual references, including quotations, to support and illustrate interpretations.

AO2: Analyse the language, form and structure used by a writer to create meanings and effects, using relevant subject terminology where appropriate.

AO3: Show understanding of the relationships between texts and the contexts in which they were written.

How these resources support you

In this book, you will develop your skills in each of the Assessment Objectives above as you:

- explore each poem in Cluster 1 and develop a focused response that will help you when it comes to comparing poems
- consider possible links between the poems and develop ways of comparing and writing about them.

POEM PAIR 1: 'WALKING AWAY' AND 'FOLLOWER'

In this section you will develop your skills in linking and comparing poems by using the following question:

Compare <u>how</u> poets present <u>attitudes towards relationships between parents and children</u> in '<u>Walking Away</u>' and **one** other poem from 'Love and relationships'.

> This reminds you that you must explain how the poets use techniques to present attitudes.

> This tells you what aspects of content you must write about.

> The 'named' poem will always be printed on the question paper.

Choosing a poem to compare

1 Which poems might be suitable to compare with 'Walking Away' to show how different poets present attitudes towards relationships between parents and children?

Remember that poems on a similar theme that have contrasting features offer good writing opportunities, just as ones with similar features do.

2 Discuss possible choices with a partner.

3 To develop your skills in preparing and writing an answer, let's say the poem you have chosen to compare with 'Walking Away' is Seamus Heaney's 'Follower'.

Reread the two poems in Cluster 1 Units 7 and 10. If you have studied these poems already and completed the focused responses, they will be very useful for your comparison, so refresh your memory.

Comparing content

1 On a sheet of paper, create two columns headed 'Walking Away' by Cecil Day-Lewis and 'Follower' by Seamus Heaney. With a partner, discuss the following aspects of each poem:

- who is speaking
- about whom
- in what situation and at what point in time
- what happens – how the situation develops
- the attitudes and feelings of the speaker towards the other person
- why you think the poet chose to write the poem.

2 Now make notes on similarities and differences between these aspects in the two columns. In particular, think about the **perspective** from which each poem is being told. Just as a hill can look a different shape when seen from different angles, experiences can look different at different points in your life and in different circumstances.

Comparing language

1 In verse one of 'Walking Away' the poet uses descriptive details that appeal to your sense of sight to help you visualise the scene, for example 'leaves just turning, / The touch-lines new-ruled'.

What examples of sense impressions (details that help you to see, hear, feel and so on) can you find in 'Follower'?

2 The poet in 'Follower' uses images, for example the simile 'His shoulders globed like a full sail strung', and the metaphor 'Mapping the furrow exactly'. How do these images create vivid impressions of the scene for the reader?

3 In 'Walking Away', what do you think the poet is trying to get the reader to imagine when he writes 'eddying away / Like a winged seed'?

4 The last six lines of 'Follower' emphasise **closeness** in the relationship between father and son. Which words and phrases suggest this? How do they suggest it?

5 Several images in 'Walking Away' suggest **separation**. Find examples, and explain how they bring out the parent's feelings.

6 In 'Follower', the father is described as an 'expert'. Which details used to describe how he works emphasise this? How do they emphasise it?

7 In 'Walking Away', which details suggest that the son is rather vulnerable and lacking in self-confidence?

8 Look at the last verse of 'Follower'. What is the effect of the rhythm created by the list, separated by commas, in 'tripping, falling, / Yapping'?

9 In 'Walking Away', the poet begins the poem by describing an experience in his past, and then quickly breaks off, interrupting his flow to describe the scene, separating 'A sunny day with the leaves just turning, / The touch-lines new-ruled' with dashes. What do you think this shows about how he remembers the day?

Comparing structure and form

These poems could be said to have similar structures. They both describe experiences and move towards a climax in which each poet reflects on the significance of the experience and concludes with a key thought – almost a 'message' – about that experience. The words 'But' and 'Perhaps' in the last two verses of the poems signal the final 'messages' for the reader.

1 Giving reasons, explain which of the following statements you most agree with.

Like a winged seed loosened from its parent stem

(From 'Walking Away')

My father worked with a horse-plough,
His shoulders globed like a full sail strung
Between the shafts and the furrow.
The horses strained at his clicking tongue.

(From 'Follower')

In the last three lines of 'Follower', the poet:

- feels resentful about his father now he has grown old
- understands that he now has responsibilities towards his father
- thinks that 'the wheel has come full circle'
- is proud that he is now a leader, not a follower.

2 Now write a sentence in which you explain the idea that the poet is expressing in the last two lines of 'Walking Away'.

3 Poets often emphasise key words and phrases by placing them at the openings of lines, using **enjambement**. For instance, in 'Follower', 'Behind' at the start of the last line stresses how the roles of father and son have changed.

In 'Walking Away', how does the placement of the following phrases make a vivid impression on the reader? What does each phrase suggest to you?

a 'Wrenched from its orbit'
b 'Into a wilderness'
c 'Gnaws at my mind still'.

4 Both poems have a regular **rhyme scheme** ('Follower' using half-rhyme rather than full rhyme). It is not always clear why poets choose particular forms in which to write. Do you agree with any of the following statements? Give reasons for your answer.

Seamus Heaney uses a regular rhyme scheme:

- to suggest the regular movement of the horse-plough
- because the poem's formal 'shape' reflects the father's precise approach to his job and the pride he takes in his work
- for no particular reason.

5 Reread 'Walking Away' and study the rhyme scheme. You will see that the poet uses alternately rhyming lines in each verse. The rhyme helps to create an emphasis on the last line of each verse – a sort of 'mini-climax'. How do the last lines of the first two verses bring out the father's feelings about his son as he watches him grow up?

Writing a comparison

Using your work on this poem, develop your skills in writing a comparison by responding to the question below, using 'Follower' as the poem to compare:

> Compare how poets present attitudes towards relationships between parents and children in 'Walking Away' and **one** other poem from 'Love and relationships'.

 Complete this assignment on Cambridge Elevate

POEM PAIR 2: 'NEUTRAL TONES' AND 'WINTER SWANS'

In this section you will develop your skills in linking and comparing poems by using the question below:

> Compare how poets present <u>attitudes towards love relationships</u> in 'Neutral Tones' and **one** other poem from 'Love and relationships'.

This reminds you that you must explain how the poets use techniques to present attitudes.

This tells you what aspects of content you must write about.

The 'named' poem will always be printed on the question paper.

Choosing a poem to compare

1 Go back to Cluster 1 Unit 5. Which poems might be suitable to compare with 'Neutral Tones' to show how different poets present attitudes towards love relationships?

Remember that poems on a similar theme that have contrasting features offer good writing opportunities, just as ones with similar features do.

2 Discuss possible choices with a partner.

3 To develop your skills in preparing and writing an answer, let's say the poem you have chosen to compare with 'Neutral Tones' is Owen Sheers's 'Winter Swans'.

Reread the two poems in Cluster 1 Units 5 and 13. If you have studied these poems already and completed the focused responses, they will be very useful for your comparison, so refresh your memory.

Comparing content

1 On a sheet of paper, create two columns headed 'Neutral Tones' by Thomas Hardy and 'Winter Swans' by Owen Sheers. With a partner, discuss the following aspects of each poem:

- who is speaking
- about what or whom

- in what situation and at what point in time
- what happens – how the situation develops
- the attitudes and feelings of the speaker towards the other person
- the atmosphere created
- why you think the poet chose to write the poem.

2 Now make notes on similarities and differences between these aspects in the two columns.

Comparing language

There is a generally more pleasant atmosphere and optimistic mood in 'Winter Swans' than in 'Neutral Tones'.

1 In two columns, list words and phrases in the Hardy poem that create a rather negative and dismal mood, and words and phrases in the Sheers poem that create a more positive and calm mood. For example:

'Neutral Tones' – negative/dismal	'Winter Swans' – positive/calm
'starving sod'	'stilling water'

And a grin of bitterness swept thereby
Like an ominous bird a-wing....

(From 'Neutral Tones')

2 Compare your lists with a partner and discuss how your chosen details are used to create atmosphere.

3 Both poets use sense impressions to make their description vivid for the reader. In 'Neutral Tones', the poet's use of descriptive detail mainly appeals to the reader's sense of sight in bringing out the drabness and melancholy of the scene, for example 'a pond edged with grayish leaves'.

In 'Winter Swans', Sheers uses more detailed and developed imagery in describing the scene. Write notes, as in the example below, explaining how these images help the reader to imagine the scene:

'the waterlogged earth / gulping for breath at our feet'	'gulping for breath' suggests the sound made by the soggy ground when trodden on
'with a show of tipping in unison.'	
'As if rolling weights down their bodies to their heads'	
'they halved themselves in the dark water, / icebergs of white feather'	
'like boats righting in rough weather.'	
'porcelain over the stilling water.'	
'I noticed our hands … / … / …folded, one over the other, / Like a pair of wings settling after flight.'	

4 Discuss your notes with a partner.

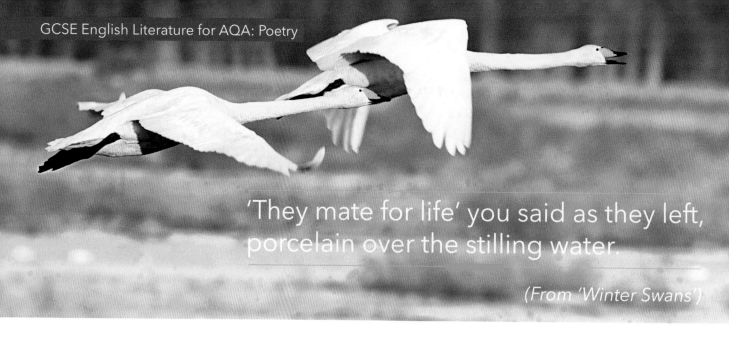

'They mate for life' you said as they left,
porcelain over the stilling water.

(From 'Winter Swans')

5 In 'Neutral Tones', Hardy describes the sun as 'white, as though chidden of God' in the opening verse and 'the God-curst sun' in the final verse. In 'Winter Swans', the whiteness of the swans is emphasised in 'icebergs of white feather'. (You might be familiar with the techniques of metaphor and symbolism.)

What do you think these forms of whiteness represent, and how do they create different feelings in the reader?

Comparing structure and form

1 'Neutral Tones' opens with a description of a dismal scene. There is a similar description in the last two lines. What does this suggest about the development of the speaker's situation?

2 There is also a description of miserable weather at the start of 'Winter Swans', but the word 'until' at the beginning of verse three signals a change in the direction of the poem. In verse two the couple are 'silent and apart'. In the last two verses the poet focuses on the lovers' hands. What do these different descriptions suggest about the development of the couple's relationship in the poem?

3 'Neutral Tones' has a regular pattern of rhyme, and the word 'And' is used at the opening of six lines.

a How do these features help to create the mood of the poem?

b The last lines of each verse are shorter than the rest and are indented. Why do you think this is?

4 'Winter Swans' is written in free verse with a shorter final verse to emphasise the calm ending.

Sheers frequently places important words and phrases at the openings of lines to emphasise them, for example 'gulping for breath'. Can you find other examples and explain how they emphasise important details?

Writing a comparison

Using your work on this poem, develop your skills in writing a comparison by responding to the question below, using 'Winter Swans' as the poem to compare:

> Compare how poets present attitudes towards love relationships in 'Neutral Tones' and **one** other poem from 'Love and relationships'.

 Complete this assignment on Cambridge Elevate

POEM PAIR 3: 'MOTHER, ANY DISTANCE' AND 'BEFORE YOU WERE MINE'

In this section you will develop your skills in linking and comparing poems by using the question below:

> Compare <u>how</u> poets present <u>attitudes towards relationships between parents and children</u> in '<u>Mother, any distance</u>' and **one** other poem from 'Love and relationships'.

> This reminds you that you must explain how the poets use techniques to present attitudes.

> This tells you what aspects of content you must write about.

> The 'named' poem will always be printed on the question paper.

Choosing a poem to compare

1 Which poems might be suitable to compare with 'Mother, any distance' to show how different poets present attitudes towards relationships between parents and children?

Remember that poems on a similar theme that have contrasting features offer good writing opportunities, just as ones with similar features do.

2 Discuss possible choices with a partner.

3 To develop your skills in preparing and writing an answer, let's say the poem you have chosen to compare with 'Mother, any distance' is Carol Ann Duffy's 'Before You Were Mine'.

Reread the two poems in Cluster 1 Units 11 and 12. If you have studied these poems already and completed the focused responses, they will be very useful for your comparison, so refresh your memory.

Comparing content

1 On a sheet of paper, create two columns headed 'Mother, any distance' by Simon Armitage and 'Before You Were Mine' by Carol Ann Duffy. With a partner, discuss the following aspects of each poem:

- who is speaking
- to whom

- in what situation and at what point in time
- what happens – how the situation develops
- the attitudes and feelings of the speaker towards the other person
- why you think the poet chose to write the poem.

2 Now make notes on similarities and differences between these aspects in the two columns. In particular, think about the perspective from which each poem is being told. Both poems describe mothers from the point of view of their children, but at what points in their lives?

3 Do the speakers in the poems admire similar or different qualities in their mothers? With a partner, discuss whether you think any of the following words might describe how the speakers see their mothers, supporting your views with details from the text:

Comparing language

1 The poet doesn't use a great variety of images in 'Mother, any distance', but he develops the idea of the unrolling tape-measure to suggest the speaker's gradual movement away from the security his mother represents. Travelling a 'distance' needs a base of support and security – 'a second pair of hands'.

Following the theme through, explain what the poet is suggesting when he uses the following words and phrases – as in the example given:

'You come to help me measure windows,'	*the mother helps him to see what he needs to do – weigh up challenges in life*
'reporting metres, centimetres back to base,'	
'feeding out, unreeling / years between us.'	
'Anchor. Kite.'	
'I space-walk'	
'to the loft, to breaking point, where something has to give;'	
'I reach / towards a hatch that opens on an endless sky / to fall or fly.'	

2 In 'Before You Were Mine', the poet uses sense impressions to bring to life the mother's youthful experiences, for example 'shriek at the pavement'. Find other examples and explain how they make the scene vivid for the reader.

Your polka-dot dress blows round your legs. Marilyn.

(From 'Before You Were Mine')

I space-walk through the empty bedrooms

(From 'Mother, any distance')

3 With a partner, discuss how the following phrases express important ideas in the poem:

a 'the fizzy, movie tomorrows / the right walk home could bring'
b 'my loud, possessive yell'
c 'your ghost clatters toward me'
d 'stamping stars from the wrong pavement'.

4 In 'Mother, any distance', Simon Armitage uses lots of words with long vowel sounds in the first two verses: 'acres', 'prairies' 'floors' 'spool', 'tape', 'metres', 'centimetres', 'base', 'feeding', 'unreeling', 'between'. He also uses lots of verbs ending in '-ing'.

a How do these word choices affect the **pace** and flow of the poem?
b How might they reinforce the central image of the unrolling tape-measure?

Comparing structure and form

1 'Mother, any distance' is written in three verses. The first begins (quite dramatically) with 'Mother', the second begins 'You' (his mother), and the third begins 'I'. Bearing in mind what you have discussed about the ideas in the poem, what do you think the change of focus in verse three suggests?

2 In the 'middle' of the poem, the poet uses the two words 'Anchor' and 'Kite', which create a concise, powerful contrast. How does the contrast at this point indicate a change in the direction of the poem?

3 The shortness of the last line 'to fall or fly', its use of contrast, and its use of alliteration create a strong climax. Why do you think that Armitage wanted to end the poem with 'fly' rather than 'fall' – he could have put them the other way round?

4 In 'Before You Were Mine', the repetition of 'before you were mine' helps the poem to finish on a strong note, and the last line has a regular rhythm, which makes it memorable. Read it aloud to appreciate the effect of the words. What final impression of the mother does the poet leave the reader with when she writes 'sparkle and waltz and laugh'?

Writing a comparison

Using your work on this poem, develop your skills in writing a comparison by responding to the question below, using 'Before You Were Mine' as the poem to compare:

> Compare how poets present attitudes towards relationships between parents and children in 'Mother, any distance' and **one** other poem from 'Love and relationships'

 Complete this assignment on Cambridge Elevate

EXAMPLE RESPONSE: 'LOVE'S PHILOSOPHY' AND 'THE FARMER'S BRIDE'

In this section you will develop your skills in linking and comparing poems by writing a response to the question below. You will then study a good example response.

> Compare how poets present attitudes towards romantic love in 'Love's Philosophy' and **one** other poem from 'Love and relationships'.

The poem chosen for comparison is Charlotte Mew's 'The Farmer's Bride'.

Making notes

The following example uses the model of annotating the 'named' poem, along with brief notes on the poem chosen from the rest of the anthology cluster. You might have a preferred way of making notes that works for you. With these notes, notice that:

- no complete sentences are used
- notes can be made very concisely when based on annotation
- no quotations are noted on the 'remembered' poem (this might take too much time and they could be added when writing).

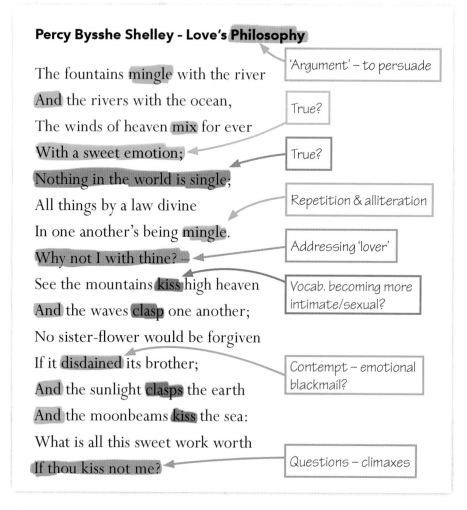

Percy Bysshe Shelley - Love's Philosophy

The fountains mingle with the river   'Argument' – to persuade
And the rivers with the ocean,
The winds of heaven mix for ever   True?
With a sweet emotion;   True?
Nothing in the world is single;
All things by a law divine   Repetition & alliteration
In one another's being mingle.
Why not I with thine? —   Addressing 'lover'
See the mountains kiss high heaven
And the waves clasp one another;   Vocab. becoming more intimate/sexual?
No sister-flower would be forgiven
If it disdained its brother;   Contempt – emotional blackmail?
And the sunlight clasps the earth
And the moonbeams kiss the sea:
What is all this sweet work worth
If thou kiss not me?   Questions – climaxes

Charlotte Mew – The Farmer's Bride

- First-person narrative

- Dialect helps create character

- Speaker already has her as wife unlike in 'L.P.' but can't satisfy sexual desires

- Nature references – adjectives to describe setting, similes for nature/behaviour of bride

- Speaker has sympathy with timid bride – but frustrated (see last verse, which focuses on appearance)

- Contrast – like hare/mouse

- Regular rhyme scheme – **couplets** create emphasis at ends of verses

- Key words and phrases emphasised at openings of lines.

Getting it into writing

1 Reread 'The Farmer's Bride' (Cluster 1 Unit 6). If you have studied these two poems already and completed the focused responses, they will be very useful for your comparison, so refresh your memory.

2 Now write your response to the question below, using 'The Farmer's Bride' as the paired poem:

> Compare how poets present attitudes towards romantic love in 'Love's Philosophy' and **one** other poem from 'Love and relationships'.

Use the notes above to help you, but add your own ideas.

You could write in timed conditions for 35 minutes (assuming you would spend about 10 minutes making notes).

Paired assessment

1 When you have completed your response, exchange it with a partner. Then answer these questions, giving examples in each case:

a   Has your partner made similar points to you?

b   Has either of you made points that the other hasn't?

c   Have all points been made clearly? If not, check what your partner intended to say.

d   Are there things you disagree about?

e   Have all points been supported by references to the poems? If not, suggest which details might have been used to back up the points you make.

f   Have all references to the poets' techniques shown the use and effect of the technique?

Now read the example response.

Example response

'Philosophy' can be defined as something like 'the study of wisdom', and implies a love of argument, and so the title of 'Love's Philosophy' sounds very 'highbrow' – which is ironic, since the speaker is addressing his 'lover' and presenting arguments that are basically designed to make their relationship more physical. In the poem, he argues that in nature lots of elements mix or mingle together, and therefore so should he and his lover. Some of his arguments are quite persuasive ('The fountains mingle with the river / And the rivers with the ocean' ✔, while others sound persuasive but perhaps aren't so convincing when examined e.g. 'The winds of heaven mix for ever / With a sweet emotion' – how can they mix with emotion? There are some sweeping statements: 'Nothing in the world is single': is this true? The speaker's tone is very confident. The phrase 'by a law divine' in verse one is an attempt to be persuasive by suggesting that God is on the side of his argument, and in verse two 'disdained' suggests that if the lady doesn't become more intimate, she could be accused of being proud and thinking herself superior.

> ✔ Points are supported by quotations/references to the text

The poem is written in a regular rhyme scheme in two verses. ✔ These are essentially two sentences presenting stages of the argument, separated by semi-colons, which makes the poem sound quite formal. The repetition of 'And' creates the impression of a relentlessly unfolding argument. Each verse ends in a shorter line in the form of a question, the second of which puts the onus on the lady to respond; 'Why not I with thine?' becomes 'If thou kiss not me?' In both verses there is alliteration and repetition of words with similar meaning for emphasis e.g. 'mix' and 'mingle'. Such words are more 'sexual' in verse two: 'kiss', 'clasp'. The speaker is becoming bolder!

> ✔ Points are organised into content/style sections

Although 'The Farmer's Bride' is also at least partly about sexual fulfilment, <u>the situation is different</u> because the farmer is actually married. The poem is a narrative told from the farmer's point of view about how he 'chose a maid' who proved to be very timid. He wonders if she was too young, and admits that he was very busy with the harvest when he wooed her, and he might have made a hasty choice. The poem moves towards a powerful climax in which the farmer describes his bride's physical attractions and his inability to demonstrate his feelings towards her: 'her eyes, her hair, her hair!' At the same time he feels pity for her: 'Alone, poor maid'. <u>Whereas the speaker in the previous poem seems confident and assured</u> (though he may be addressing the lady in a 'tongue-in-cheek' manner!), <u>the farmer appears rather downcast and bewildered</u>.

> Notice that the writer found more differences than similarities

Unlike Shelley, Mew uses a lot of similes taken from nature to describe the maid as if she is a simple creature. When she runs away she is described as 'flying like a hare', showing her desperation to escape, contrasting with 'like a mouse' and 'shy as a leveret', which show her fear. The farmer speaks a form of dialect (e.g. 'when us was wed'), which creates an informal tone and suggests that he is a simple country farmer. <u>Whereas Shelley presents ideas in an abstract way, Mew describes the country setting in detail</u>, particularly in the second to last verse, using such phrases as 'A magpie's spotted feathers'. Although the poem is written in a regular rhyme scheme, the poet often emphasises key words and phrases at the openings of lines e.g. 'Betwixt us' and 'As well as most'.

> Notice the paragraph structure is:
> • Poem 1 content
> • Poem 1 style
> • Poem 2 content
> • Poem 2 style.
>
> Another good option would be:
> • Poem 1 content
> • Poem 2 content
> • Poem 1 style
> • Poem 2 style.

2 An example response is not a 'perfect' model answer. Use the questions you applied to your partner's response earlier, and decide whether aspects of this response could be improved.

Power and conflict
1 Ozymandias

GETTING STARTED – THE POEM AND YOU

Look at the pictures. These are places that once represented power. What are they now?

GETTING CLOSER – FOCUS ON DETAILS

First impressions

1 Read 'Ozymandias'. Which of these statements best fits the poem?

The poem is about:

a   the remains of a statue in the desert
b   a fallen tyrant from long ago
c   the vanity of a long-forgotten ruler
d   how all things, however great, decay with time.

2 Write a sentence using parts of these phrases to sum up what you think the poem is about.

Interpreting themes, ideas, attitudes and feelings

1 What do we know – or what can we deduce – about the statue, the ruler and the sculptor? Make a table like this to organise your ideas and use evidence from the poem to **justify** your responses:

	What we know	What we might deduce
The statue		
The ruler		
The sculptor		

2 Discuss your findings with a partner or as a class, then use the notes from the table to help you write a couple of sentences about each of these: the statue, the ruler and the sculptor.

3 How far can you be sure of any of the 'facts' here? Can you trust the sculptor to have made an accurate likeness? Or trust the traveller to have relayed correct information? Or the poet to have communicated accurately what the traveller reported? Does it matter?

OZYMANDIAS

I met a traveller from an antique land
Who said: Two vast and trunkless legs of stone
Stand in the desert … Near them, on the sand,
Half sunk, a shattered visage lies, whose frown,
And wrinkled lip, and sneer of cold command,   5
Tell that its sculptor well those passions read
Which yet survive, stamped on these lifeless things,
The hand that mocked them, and the heart that fed:
And on the pedestal these words appear:
'My name is Ozymandias, king of kings: 10
Look on my works, ye Mighty, and despair!'
Nothing beside remains. Round the decay
Of that colossal wreck, boundless and bare
The lone and level sands stretch far away.

Percy Bysshe Shelley

antique land (1): ancient country (in this case, Egypt)
trunkless (2): without a body
visage (4): face
pedestal (9): plinth or base on which a statue stands

 Listen to the poem on Cambridge Elevate

97

PUTTING DETAILS TO USE

Analysing language, form and structure

1 This is the only example of a **sonnet** in this cluster. With a partner, find out what a sonnet is or revise what you already know. Jot down some notes about the:

- number of lines
- length of the lines
- **rhythm** of the lines
- rhyme pattern.

2 Where does 'Ozymandias' keep to the sonnet **form** and where does it depart from it?

3 To make yourself more familiar with the poem, look at the following version, which is out of sequence, and see how far you can reconstruct it. Work with a partner and try to avoid looking at the original!

A And on the pedestal these words appear:

B And wrinkled lip and sneer of cold command

C Half sunk, a shatter'd visage lies, whose frown,

D I met a traveller from an antique land

E Look on my works, ye Mighty, and despair!'

F 'My name is Ozymandias, king of kings:

G Nothing beside remains. Round the decay

H Of that colossal wreck, boundless and bare,

I Stand in the desert. Near them, on the sand,

J Tell that its sculptor well those passions read

K The hand that mock'd them and the heart that fed;

L The lone and level sands stretch far away.

M Which yet survive, stamped on these lifeless things,

N Who said: Two vast and trunkless legs of stone

Contexts

This is Shelley's most famous sonnet, and one of the best known in English literature, although it does not stick strictly to the 'rules' of the usual sonnet form. But then, Shelley was a rebel against many of the conventions of his time, and his poetry is no exception!

This poem was written in 1817. The historical **context** is the archaeological finds that had just been made in Egypt, which were Shelley's inspiration. Ozymandias was another name for the Egyptian pharaoh Rameses II. The poem explores the idea that, with the passing of time, all great rulers and empires, however powerful they may have once been, will crumble like a statue.

4 Now look at the key words in the poem out of context. Pick out those that have a negative association and those that have a positive one. Any others, which you can ignore, will be neutral. Make a list and, where necessary, add a note to explain your thinking, for example although 'antique' could mean 'valuable', you might put it under 'negative' because it implies 'out of date'.

words	appear	lip	pedestal
cold	half	sunk	wrinkled
lies	visage	frown	traveller
antique	land	look	shattered
works	Mighty	despair	Ozymandias
king	kings	survive	boundless
name	beside	legs	colossal
round	decay	wreck	sculptor
bare	stand	desert	passions
near	sand	well	stamped
mocked	read	hand	lifeless
heart	fed	lone	trunkless
level	sands	stretch	nothing
far	away	vast	remains
stone	sneer		

Learning checkpoint

Write a few sentences (about 100–150 words) to show how Shelley manages to communicate a negative impression of the king, Ozymandias.

Show your skills

Look at the following piece of writing. It answers the question: **How does Shelley use language to convey a negative impression of the king?**

Annotate the text to pick out:

a how the student organises the answer
b where it is explaining/describing
c where it goes further and explores or **interprets** the words of the poem.

Shelley conveys a negative impression of Ozymandias in several ways. Firstly, he describes how the face of the king is shattered and half sunk in the sand, which is a poor place for any 'mighty' ruler. Secondly, the face shows a sneer and a frown – not very nice characteristics. Not only does the face sneer, it sneers with cold command, looking down on its subjects. Thirdly, we notice that the sculptor mocked the king's character, showing that not all his subjects respected him. Finally, his egocentric words 'look on my works, ye Mighty, and despair' are mocked by time, as there is nothing left to see of his works, only sand. There is also an element of ridicule in the poem shown in the **contrast** of the haughty words and the reality that 'nothing beside remains' and also in the absurd sight of two legs sticking up with no body attached.

Two vast and trunkless legs of stone
Stand in the desert.

GETTING IT INTO WRITING

Comparing poems

In this activity you will not be comparing 'Ozymandias' with another poem from the cluster, but with a poem that was written about the same thing. This will give you useful practice in the technique of comparison writing – and in dealing with a poem you have not seen before.

Another poet, Horace Smith, travelled with Shelley on his trip to Egypt. Smith also wrote a poem about the broken statue:

On a Stupendous Leg of Granite, Discovered Standing by Itself in the Deserts of Egypt, with the Inscription Inserted Below

In Egypt's sandy silence, all alone,
Stands a gigantic Leg, which far off throws
The only shadow that the Desert knows.
'I am great Ozymandias,' saith the stone,
'The King of kings: this mighty city shows
The wonders of my hand.' The city's gone!
Naught but the leg remaining to disclose
The site of that forgotten Babylon.
We wonder, and some hunter may express
Wonder like ours, when through the wilderness
Where London stood, holding the wolf in chase,
He meets some fragment huge, and stops to guess
What wonderful, but unrecorded, race
Once dwelt in that annihilated place.

Write a comparison of the two poems, paying particular attention to language and theme.

Your response

In what ways is the poem 'Ozymandias' still relevant to us today?

Power and conflict

2 London

GETTING STARTED – THE POEM AND YOU

What impressions do you have of London, whether or not you have been there or live there?

Write down three adjectives to describe your impressions. You may want to choose some of these, or think of your own:

busy	dirty	modern	interesting
old	bustling	exciting	crowded

GETTING CLOSER – FOCUS ON DETAILS

First impressions

1. Read or listen to the poem.

   Which words stay in your head after a first reading or hearing? Put the poem to one side and write down all the words or phrases you remember.

2. Compare this list with a partner and note which words you both have. You could then compile a list as a class.

3. Look at the most frequently remembered words and phrases. What associations do they have? For example 'manacles' might bring to mind prison, chains, punishment, heavy weights and so on.

Interpreting themes, ideas, attitudes and feelings

1. Reread the poem, looking more closely at the language used and in particular the nouns. For example 'cry' appears three times, used as a noun.

2. Sort the nouns into three categories: positive, neutral and negative. For example:

Positive	Neutral	Negative
	infant	manacles

Some words can be interpreted in different ways – blood, for example. You might want to put these words into more than one category.

You may not yet have a clear idea of what the poem is saying but you will have a clear notion of its general **tone** and attitude.

 Contexts

William Blake (1757–1827) is now recognised as an important figure in the Romantic period, although he was virtually ignored during his lifetime. He was both a poet and an artist. Like Shelley, he was a radical thinker with political views that were unusual at the time. He rejected established religion and was against oppression by the Church and state. Blake lived in London, and saw around him the poverty and social problems caused by the Industrial Revolution. This is one of his best-known poems.

LONDON

I wander through each chartered street,
Near where the chartered Thames does flow,
And mark in every face I meet
Marks of weakness, marks of woe.

In every cry of every man,   5
In every infant's cry of fear,
In every voice, in every ban,
The mind-forged manacles I hear:

How the chimney-sweeper's cry
Every black'ning church appalls,   10
And the hapless soldier's sigh
Runs in blood down palace walls.

But most through midnight streets I hear
How the youthful harlot's curse
Blasts the new-born infant's tear,   15
And blights with plagues the marriage hearse.

William Blake

manacles (8): metal bands
or shackles, used to fasten
the hands or feet of a
prisoner
harlot (14): prostitute

 Listen to the poem on Cambridge Elevate

PUTTING DETAILS TO USE

Analysing language, form and structure

1 Now annotate a copy of the poem to explain unfamiliar words and your initial ideas. For example:

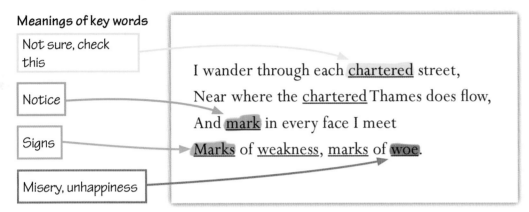

Meanings of key words

Not sure, check this

Notice

Signs

Misery, unhappiness

I wander through each chartered street,
Near where the chartered Thames does flow,
And mark in every face I meet
Marks of weakness, marks of woe.

Notes and thoughts

Repetition of 'chartered' (why?) and of 'mark' 3 times

Alliteration 'weakness'/'woe'

Sees unhappiness wherever he goes

Repetition gives a plodding, dreary feel

Make a note of any words or phrases you don't understand and research them when you have the opportunity.

2 The form of the poem is obvious, with its four-line verses rhyming ABAB and four beats in each line. However, the last verse seems slightly different. Read it aloud and see if you can work out how it varies.

 Learning checkpoint

What is Blake's problem? Why has he written this pessimistic description of London? Take a look at the poem as a whole. The first **verse** might be summed up like this:

- Everywhere he goes through London's streets, he sees signs of misery.

Now read the following summaries of the other verses and arrange them in order from the most convincing to the least convincing. You may wish to combine some parts of them to make your own summary.

Verse two

a In everyone's voices, he hears evidence of mental oppression.

b He notices signs of self-imposed chains in the sounds that people make.

c He sees that everyone, whether young or old, lacks freedom.

Verse three

a The chimney sweep's suffering shocks the Church; the soldier's suffering is marked in blood on palace walls.

b The Church should be appalled by chimney sweeps' cries and those in palaces should be aware of people's suffering.

c Church and state need to take notice of the cries of the people, young and old.

Verse four

a But most of all, at night he hears the curses of young mothers, prostitutes whose real or metaphorical diseases will infect both children and marriage.

b Even babies suffer from the sins of their parents, and marriage is seen as leading to death rather than renewal.

c The worst thing is the curse of the prostitute, which scars the newborn and marriage itself.

Show your skills

Write a few sentences (between 100 and 150 words) to describe how Blake sees London. Try to get at the feelings that lie underneath what he says.

You might wish to use some of these guiding phrases:

Blake sees London as a place of restraint and …

Each face he sees reminds him of …

All, young and old, suffer from …

In particular he is angry about … He blames …

Finally, he despairs that …

GETTING IT INTO WRITING

Blake uses many memorable phrases in this poem. Write a sentence or two about each of the following, exploring how they add to the power of the poem:

a 'mind-forged manacles'
b 'youthful harlot's curse'
c 'marriage hearse'.

Comparing poems

'London' focuses more on the notion of 'power' rather than 'conflict'. Here we can see how the rich and powerful have control of the city (the river and the streets) and, Blake hints, control of the minds of the citizens. Church and palace have it in their power to ease the situation of the exploited (poor chimney sweeps, hapless soldiers) but do nothing. The powerlessness of the people affects even their personal relationships and turns future opportunity into despair.

As you work your way through the cluster, notice which other poems use power as part of the poem's theme.

GETTING CREATIVE

Writing a parody (an imitation of a writer's style) is a powerful way to really get to know a piece of writing. Try writing a verse (or more) about London or any other town or city in the style of Blake but from a 21st-century point of view. For example:

I cycle through each noisy street

Near where the Underground appears

And all pedestrians I meet

Have a device plugged in their ears.

Your response

Are there any similarities between 'London' and life in big cities now – both here and abroad? How might Blake view the enormous cities of South America, Africa and Asia with their accompanying shanty towns? Or the conditions in towns where factories have closed and opportunities for work have disappeared?

Explore the poem further with a video activity on Cambridge Elevate

And mark in every face I meet
Marks of weakness, marks of woe.

Power and conflict

3 The Prelude

GETTING STARTED – THE POEM AND YOU

Many people are afraid of the dark, especially young children. Why do you think this is?

What associations does darkness/night have? Can you think of any ghost stories that take place in broad daylight?

GETTING CLOSER – FOCUS ON DETAILS

First impressions

1 Read the poem. Then read the following summary, choosing what you think are the most appropriate words where there is a choice:

The boy steals/borrows/takes a boat and rows out into the lake. He rows slowly/skilfully/lustily, keeping a straight course by aiming for a ridge's summit/ huge peak/grim shape. The growing size of one of the peaks terrifies/unnerves/disturbs him and he turns around. He leaves the boat where he found it and returns home, but for days afterwards is disturbed by nightmares/ghostly images/dark thoughts.

2 Compare your choices with a partner and agree on a version of the text. Some of the choices are quite close in meaning, so you are not trying to find the right answer but the best answer. If you think that there is anything important missing from the summary, expand it.

3 Share your choices with the rest of the class and agree on a summary.

Interpreting themes, ideas, attitudes and feelings

In groups of four, discuss the following statements. Decide how far you agree with them on a scale of 1 to 5, where 1 is 'not at all' and 5 is 'strongly agree'.

a The boy feels guilty for stealing the boat and the grim shapes of the mountains appear to reinforce his guilt.

b When you are on your own and it's dark, ordinary sights and sounds can seem more powerful or mysterious.

c The boy is overwhelmed by the power of nature and feels insignificant.

d The strange feelings he experienced that night have haunted him ever since.

Contexts

William Wordsworth (1770–1850) was one of the first writers whose work was labelled as 'Romantic'. Much of his poetry is about humanity's relationship with nature, inspired by the English Lake District, where he spent most of his life. The Romantic poets helped change how people thought about the natural world. They believed that mankind does not control nature; it's the other way round. This extract is from Wordsworth's long autobiographical poem 'The Prelude', which was not published until after his death. In the extract, the poet is 'led by her'– that is, by nature – to the experience he describes.

One summer evening (led by her) I found
A little boat tied to a willow tree
Within a rocky cove, its usual home.
Straight I unloosed her chain, and stepping in
Pushed from the shore. It was an act of stealth   5
And troubled pleasure, nor without the voice
Of mountain-echoes did my boat move on;
Leaving behind her still, on either side,
Small circles glittering idly in the moon,
Until they melted all into one track   10
Of sparkling light. But now, like one who rows,
Proud of his skill, to reach a chosen point
With an unswerving line, I fixed my view
Upon the summit of a craggy ridge,
The horizon's utmost boundary; far above   15
Was nothing but the stars and the grey sky.
She was an elfin pinnace; lustily
I dipped my oars into the silent lake,
And, as I rose upon the stroke, my boat
Went heaving through the water like a swan;   20
When, from behind that craggy steep till then
The horizon's bound, a huge peak, black and huge,
As if with voluntary power instinct,

Upreared its head. I struck and struck again,
And growing still in stature the grim shape   25
Towered up between me and the stars, and still,
For so it seemed, with purpose of its own
And measured motion like a living thing,
Strode after me. With trembling oars I turned,
And through the silent water stole my way   30
Back to the covert of the willow tree;
There in her mooring-place I left my bark, –
And through the meadows homeward went, in
     grave
And serious mood; but after I had seen
That spectacle, for many days, my brain   35
Worked with a dim and undetermined sense
Of unknown modes of being; o'er my thoughts
There hung a darkness, call it solitude
Or blank desertion. No familiar shapes
Remained, no pleasant images of trees,   40
Of sea or sky, no colours of green fields;
But huge and mighty forms, that do not live
Like living men, moved slowly through the mind
By day, and were a trouble to my dreams.

William Wordsworth

elfin (17): small or fairy-like
pinnace (17): small rowing
boat
**As if with voluntary power
instinct** (23): as if alive
bark (32): boat
undetermined (36):
uncertain, hard to pin down

 Listen to the poem on Cambridge Elevate

PUTTING DETAILS TO USE

Analysing language, form and structure

1 Like some other poems in this cluster, this extract is written using lines of ten syllables with a regular pattern of strong and weak beats in each line. What is this called?

2 Unlike, for example, 'Ozymandias', the poem is unrhymed. The name for this form, using the five beat rhythm, is **blank verse**. It is often used in epic poems about mighty subjects, but here it is used to describe the very personal experiences of growing up. This incident stands alone as a story from Wordsworth's youth although it is part of what is, in fact, Wordsworth's autobiography in verse.

3 This extract can be divided into two parts – positive and negative.

   a Where is there a hint of negativity in the first part?
   b Where would you locate the point where it changes?
   c In which lines (around this point) is there a slight upset to the rhythm?

4 Taking one section of a copy of the poem, mark words or phrases that strike you as either positive or negative. For example using yellow for positive associations and blue for negative associations:

> One summer evening (led by her) I found
> A little boat tied to a willow tree
> Within a rocky cove, its usual home.
> Straight I unloosed her chain, and stepping in
> Pushed from the shore. It was an act of stealth
> And troubled pleasure, nor without the voice
> Of mountain-echoes did my boat move on;
> Leaving behind her still, on either side,
> Small circles glittering idly in the moon,
> Until they melted all into one track
> Of sparkling light.

Work with a partner to discuss which words convey a positive, negative or neutral meaning depending on context. For example, is 'a huge peak, black and huge' necessarily negative?

Learning checkpoint

Wordsworth was a close observer of natural things yet there is very little description of nature in this long extract. Write three or four sentences to show where he does describe natural things and give your opinion about how effective those descriptions are.

Show your skills

Look at this student's annotation of a short section of the poem. Where do you think it shows evidence of exploring the text rather than just describing?

Rowed quickly – repetition shows panic

Feels relentless – it won't give up, which is why he turns and flees

Here, though, looking back and saying that it only seemed like this

> I struck and struck again,
> And growing still in stature the grim shape
> Towered up between me and the stars, and still,
> For so it seemed, with purpose of its own
> And measured motion like a living thing,
> Strode after me.

Mountain seems to be getting bigger – due to the effects of perspective but to him it looks threatening

The measured motion is like that of a human or animal taking regular steps. Use of **personification** – the mountain peaks have become threatening beings, like monsters.

GETTING IT INTO WRITING

Write a paragraph or two (about 100 words) explaining the moods and feelings of the writer and how they change as the poem progresses. You may wish to use these starting points:

At the beginning of the poem, the boy feels …

As he begins to row, he …

As he rows further, he notices …

He returns home feeling …

For sometime after that, he …

To sum up, we can see that his feelings change from …

Small circles glittering idly in the moon,
Until they melted all into one track
Of sparkling light.

Comparing poems

This poem extract is quite clearly a **narrative** – it is telling a story. Choose another poem from this cluster that also tells a story and compare the two.

What do the two poems have in common and where do they differ? In each case, think about:

- who is telling the story – and why
- what form the poet uses and how have they adapted it
- significant language features, such as notable vocabulary, **images**, other **poetic devices**
- the themes of the poem and the attitudes of the writer
- your personal response.

Your response

This passage from 'The Prelude' comes just before the section on stealing the boat:

How strange that all
The terrors, pains, and early miseries,
Regrets, vexations, lassitudes interfused
Within my mind, should e'er have borne a part,
And that a needful part, in making up
The calm existence that is mine when I
Am worthy of myself! Praise to the end!
Thanks to the means which Nature deigned to employ;
Whether her fearless visitings, or those
That came with soft alarm, like hurtless light
Opening the peaceful clouds; or she may use
Severer interventions, ministry
More palpable, as best might suit her aim.

Wordsworth is implying that 'Nature' was trying to teach him a lesson, to educate him in an important way. Does this affect the way that you respond to the poem?

GETTING CREATIVE

Another famous autobiography in verse is John Betjeman's 'Summoned by Bells'. Here is an extract:

Walking from school is a consummate art:
Which routes to follow to avoid the gangs,
Which paths to find that lead, circuitous,
To leafy squirrel haunts and plopping ponds,
For dreams of Archibald and Tiger Tim;
Which hiding-place is safe, and when it is;
What time to leave to dodge the enemy.
I only once was trapped. I knew the trap –
I heard it in their tones: 'Walk back with us.'
I knew they weren't my friends; but that soft voice
Wheedled me from my route to cold Swain's Lane.
There in a holly bush they threw me down,
Pulled off my shorts, and laughed and ran away;
And, as I struggled up, I saw grey brick,
The cemetery railings and the tombs.

Perhaps you have done something similar to Wordsworth – like taking a day off school, borrowing something without permission … Why not write about it in **free verse** – or even try blank verse, like Wordsworth or Betjeman. For example:

The day I bunked off school was hot and dry

And when I saw the sky I couldn't face

The thought of chemistry and maths. I felt

That I deserved a day to get a tan

And so I made my way …

Power and conflict
4 My Last Duchess

GETTING STARTED – THE POEM AND YOU

When someone tells a story or repeats some gossip, they often reveal something about themselves in the way they speak.

Think about conversations you have with friends and those that you have with teachers or parents. Perhaps you tell them things in a way that suits you – perhaps you miss out certain things and add others?

This poem is an example of someone telling a story and revealing a lot about himself in the process!

GETTING CLOSER – FOCUS ON DETAILS

First impressions

 1 Read 'My Last Duchess'. This is a long poem, so your first impressions may not be complete. Two characters are portrayed – the Duke, who is speaking, and the Duchess, whose portrait they are looking at.

What first impression do you get of:

a   the Duke
b   the Duchess?

Make two lists. Use any of the words below and add others of your own.

proud	powerful	generous
cultured	gentle	haughty
friendly	possessive	naïve
ruthless	happy	powerless
ungrateful	suspicious	insensitive
light-hearted		

ℹ️ Contexts

Robert Browning (1812–1889) was a very popular Victorian poet. He is best known for his **dramatic monologues** – poems that tell a story, written in character, (see 'Porphyria's Lover' in Cluster 1 Unit 3 for another example by Browning).

The narrator of 'My Last Duchess' was in fact a real historical figure – Alonso, the Duke of the Italian city of Ferrara in the years 1559 to 1597. The Duchess he is looking at in the painting was the first of his three wives, Lucrezia de' Medici, who died only two years after their marriage, in suspicious circumstances. There were rumours that she had been poisoned. In the poem, the Duke is showing her portrait to a messenger from his next wife's father.

MY LAST DUCHESS

Ferrara

That's my last Duchess painted on the wall,
Looking as if she were alive. I call
That piece a wonder, now: Fra Pandolf's hands
Worked busily a day, and there she stands.
Will't please you sit and look at her? I said 5
'Fra Pandolf' by design, for never read
Strangers like you that pictured countenance,
The depth and passion of its earnest glance,
But to myself they turned (since none puts by
The curtain I have drawn for you, but I) 10
And seemed as they would ask me, if they durst,
How such a glance came there; so, not the first
Are you to turn and ask thus. Sir, 'twas not
Her husband's presence only, called that spot
Of joy into the Duchess' cheek: perhaps 15
Fra Pandolf chanced to say 'Her mantle laps
Over my lady's wrist too much,' or 'Paint
Must never hope to reproduce the faint
Half-flush that dies along her throat': such stuff
Was courtesy, she thought, and cause enough 20
For calling up that spot of joy. She had
A heart — how shall I say? — too soon made glad,
Too easily impressed; she liked whate'er
She looked on, and her looks went everywhere.
Sir, 'twas all one! My favour at her breast, 25
The dropping of the daylight in the West,
The bough of cherries some officious fool
Broke in the orchard for her, the white mule
She rode with round the terrace — all and each
Would draw from her alike the approving
   speech, 30
Or blush, at least. She thanked men, — good! but
   thanked

Somehow — I know not how — as if she ranked
My gift of a nine-hundred-years-old name
With anybody's gift. Who'd stoop to blame
This sort of trifling? Even had you skill 35
In speech — (which I have not) — to make your
   will
Quite clear to such an one, and say, 'Just this
Or that in you disgusts me; here you miss,
Or there exceed the mark' — and if she let
Herself be lessoned so, nor plainly set 40
Her wits to yours, forsooth, and made excuse,
— E'en then would be some stooping; and I
   choose
Never to stoop. Oh sir, she smiled, no doubt,
Whene'er I passed her; but who passed without
Much the same smile? This grew; I gave
   commands; 45
Then all smiles stopped together. There she
   stands
As if alive. Will't please you rise? We'll meet
The company below, then. I repeat,
The Count your master's known munificence
Is ample warrant that no just pretence 50
Of mine for dowry will be disallowed;
Though his fair daughter's self, as I avowed
At starting, is my object. Nay, we'll go
Together down, sir. Notice Neptune, though,
Taming a sea-horse, thought a rarity, 55
Which Claus of Innsbruck cast in bronze for me!

Robert Browning

durst (11): dare
mantle (16): sleeveless cloak or shawl
officious (27): assertive or domineering
forsooth (41): indeed
munificence (49): great generosity

🔊 **Listen to the poem on Cambridge Elevate**

Interpreting themes, ideas, attitudes and feelings

1 Taking one section of the poem, work with a partner to summarise the content of that section and comment on what it shows about the Duke. You might also add any queries. For example:

The text	Summary	Comments & queries
That's my last Duchess painted on the wall, Looking as if she were alive. I call That piece a wonder, now: Fra Pandolf's hands Worked busily a day, and there she stands. Will't please you sit and look at her? I said 'Fra Pandolf' by design, for never read Strangers like you that pictured countenance, The depth and passion of its earnest glance, But to myself they turned (since none puts by The curtain I have drawn for you, but I) And seemed as they would ask me, if they durst, How such a glance came there; so, not the first Are you to turn and ask thus.	The Duke shows off the painting of his 'last Duchess' painted by Fra Pandolf. Strangers do not usually see the picture as it is behind a curtain. People who see it want to know how the painter created such a powerful expression.	The Duke is proud of the painting but he is possessive of it. He emphasises that he alone has access to it. The expression is clearly important to him. (Why?) (What has the visitor asked?)

2 Combine your summaries, comments and queries as a class. Work together to build up the sequence of events that have led up to this viewing of the painting.

3 Write a three- or four-sentence summary of these events. You may want to use or adapt some of the following sentences and then arrange them into the best order to describe what happened:

- Eventually he had her killed but he is nevertheless proud of her portrait.
- He is now looking for his next Duchess.
- She did not appreciate her husband's status and did not behave in a way he approved of.
- The Duchess behaved in a way the Duke disliked.
- The Duke would not condescend to try to correct her.
- The Duke's wife was too friendly with everyone.

4 Finally, work with a partner or in a small group to arrange these descriptions of the themes of the poem in a diamond shape (1-2-3-2-1) with the most appropriate at the top and the least appropriate at the bottom:

domestic violence	marriage breakdown	arrogance of power
know your place	love and hate	a cold-blooded killer
love of status	aristocratic evil	death of innocence

5 Discuss your ideas as a class to see which description seems to be the most fitting. It may be that someone will come up with a term that is better than any of these!

PUTTING DETAILS TO USE

Analysing language, form and structure

The form that Browning has chosen is one that he made famous: the dramatic monologue. In this form, one person speaks and both tells of an event and reveals a great deal about him or herself in the process.

The poem is written in rhyming **couplets** with a regular rhythm – do you recognise it (see 'Ozymandias')?

1 In spite of the regularity, Browning ensures that the rhyme and rhythm do not become too repetitive and tiresome. How does he do this?

2 Browning's choice of language works together with his punctuation to create a sense of active speech. The stops and starts and the repetitions all contribute to this effect. The visitor does not get to say much, but there are points where it seems he may have asked a question or made a comment. Read through and see where these might be.

 Learning checkpoint

The Duke is a self-important character anxious to show off his power and his taste in art. Pick out three instances of where he reveals more about himself than he might realise and explain the reasons for your choices.

Show your skills

Look at this example of a response to short quotations from the poem. Where does it show that the writer is analysing and/or exploring rather than simply reporting?

> She thanked men, – good! but thanked
> Somehow – I know not how – as if she ranked
> My gift of a nine-hundred-years-old name
> With anybody's gift.

Here we see the Duke revealing more of his character than he intends. He says 'good' as if to show how reasonable he is, but then goes on to show how vain he is about having inherited a title as if merely marrying him was a huge privilege. He interrupts himself as if he is spluttering with indignation. He does not understand how his wife could not worship and admire him – and he takes it for granted that his listener will agree with him.

The bough of cherries some officious fool
Broke in the orchard for her

GETTING IT INTO WRITING

How does the Duke reveal his character in his **monologue**? Write two or three paragraphs (about 150–200 words). Each paragraph should take a different aspect of his character, referring to the text. A final paragraph should give your personal comments.

Comparing poems

Both 'My Last Duchess' and 'Ozymandias' are about power, especially power wielded by an individual over others. Read 'Ozymandias' again and then write a few paragraphs comparing the two poems. When preparing your answer, you could make some rough notes in the form of a table. For example:

	'Ozymandias'	'My Last Duchess'
Form and **structure**	Sonnet – with variations …	
Language and imagery		Conversational but quite formal …
Content	The king is shown to be …	
Themes and ideas		Power is shown as …
Your response	I find Shelley's poem …	

Remember to refer to the words in the poem as you write, but do not include lengthy quotations.

GETTING CREATIVE

1 The Duke is talking to an envoy from a count, trying to negotiate his next marriage.

    a   What will the envoy be thinking?
    b   What will he report to his employer?

You could complete these as writing activities or (in response to 1b) as an improvised **dialogue** between two people.

2 A further writing activity – perhaps a dramatic monologue – would be to imagine the story told from the Duchess's point of view, either just before her death or looking back as a ghost.

Your response

Where could you imagine a similar incident happening in the 20th or 21st centuries? Who would have the unchallenged power that the Duke has, which enables him to get away with murder? Is there any situation in which the gender roles might be reversed?

Power and conflict
5 The Charge of the Light Brigade

GETTING STARTED – THE POEM AND YOU

Read the poem. How does a poem about horses, sabres and cannon affect you?
Which of these statements comes closest to describing your reaction?

a   It was a long while ago – it doesn't have anything to do with the 21st century.
b   War is horrific, whenever it takes place.
c   It's exciting; battles were different then – more heroic.
d   It's like a painting or a film – it seems colourful but not much to do with me.
e   There are still things like this happening.

ⓘ Contexts

'The Charge of the Light Brigade' tells the story of a famous charge during one of the battles of the Crimean War in 1854. A confusion in the orders relayed to the brigade led to the lightly armoured cavalry unit charging a battery of guns in a hopeless attack.

More precisely, the poem is the writer's reaction to that story when it was reported in the newspapers of the day. Similar feelings to those expressed by Tennyson were felt by some people during

the First World War and have been felt by many people since. The poetry of Wilfred Owen, among others, empathises with soldiers and celebrates their bravery and stoicism, while being critical of higher-ranked officers and the war in general.

There are also parallels in 21st-century wars, for example if we think of the sympathy many people have for soldiers sent to Iraq or Afghanistan, while wondering about the wisdom of the conflicts taking place.

GETTING CLOSER – FOCUS ON DETAILS

Interpreting themes, ideas, attitudes and feelings

Which of the sentences below do you think best describes the poet's attitude? You can adapt the sentences if you wish:

a   The actions of the soldiers were heroic but they were badly outnumbered.
b   The brigade was sent into action because they were ordered to.
c   The men suffered many casualties because of a mistake.
d   It was a glorious charge but the orders were wrong.

THE CHARGE OF THE LIGHT BRIGADE

1.

Half a league, half a league,
Half a league onward,
All in the valley of Death
   Rode the six hundred.
'Forward, the Light Brigade!   5
Charge for the guns!' he said:
Into the valley of Death
   Rode the six hundred.

2.

'Forward, the Light Brigade!'
Was there a man dismay'd?   10
Not tho' the soldier knew
   Some one had blunder'd:
Theirs not to make reply,
Theirs not to reason why,
Theirs but to do and die: 15
Into the valley of Death
   Rode the six hundred.

3.

Cannon to right of them,
Cannon to left of them,
Cannon in front of them   20
   Volley'd and thunder'd;
Storm'd at with shot and shell,
Boldly they rode and well,
Into the jaws of Death,
Into the mouth of Hell   25
   Rode the six hundred.

4.

Flash'd all their sabres bare,
Flash'd as they turn'd in air
Sabring the gunners there,
Charging an army, while   30
   All the world wonder'd:
Plunged in the battery-smoke
Right thro' the line they broke;
Cossack and Russian
Reel'd from the sabre-stroke   35
   Shatter'd and sunder'd.
Then they rode back, but not
   Not the six hundred.

🔊 **Listen to the poem on Cambridge Elevate**

5.

Cannon to right of them,
Cannon to left of them,   40
Cannon behind them
    Volley'd and thunder'd;
Storm'd at with shot and shell,
While horse and hero fell,
They that had fought so well   45
Came thro' the jaws of Death
Back from the mouth of Hell,
All that was left of them,
    Left of six hundred.

6.

When can their glory fade?   50
O the wild charge they made!
    All the world wonder'd.
Honour the charge they made!
Honour the Light Brigade,
    Noble six hundred!   55

Alfred Lord Tennyson

PUTTING DETAILS TO USE

Analysing language, form and structure

1 Explore Tennyson's use of language by using a copy of the poem to annotate
verses two, three or five. In the following example, which uses verse five, the
student has done three things:

- **a** noted interesting uses of language
- **b** commented on their purpose or effect
- **c** added personal comments (for example 'seems to be there ...').

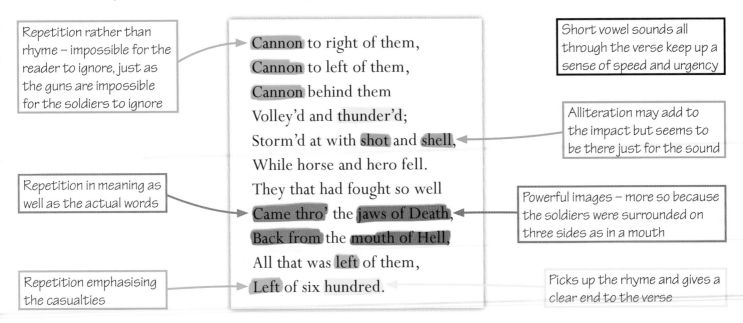

Repetition rather than rhyme – impossible for the reader to ignore, just as the guns are impossible for the soldiers to ignore

Repetition in meaning as well as the actual words

Repetition emphasising the casualties

Short vowel sounds all through the verse keep up a sense of speed and urgency

Alliteration may add to the impact but seems to be there just for the sound

Powerful images – more so because the soldiers were surrounded on three sides as in a mouth

Picks up the rhyme and gives a clear end to the verse

Cannon to right of them,
Cannon to left of them,
Cannon behind them
Volley'd and thunder'd;
Storm'd at with shot and shell,
While horse and hero fell.
They that had fought so well
Came thro' the jaws of Death,
Back from the mouth of Hell,
All that was left of them,
Left of six hundred.

2 The poem is impossible to read in a calm, quiet way. What techniques does Tennyson use to force us to read the poem 'at a gallop'?

3 'The Charge of the Light Brigade' had a big impact when it was first published six weeks after the event and the words still carry a lot of power. The poem shows that powerful writing does not depend on the extensive use of adjectives. Even the phrase 'six hundred' is treated as a noun: 'the six hundred'. Notice how 'valley of Death' (two nouns) has a stronger effect than the use of an adjective and noun (for example 'deathly valley').

Look through the poem and see how many adjectives you can find. Compare your list with that of a partner. How important are those few adjectives?

Learning checkpoint

Look back at the poem and ask yourself – is this a poem glorifying war or warning of the horrors of war? Using a copy of the poem, underline or circle any words and phrases that help you to answer the question.

Show your skills

'The Charge of the Light Brigade' has been criticised for glorifying war and the duty to die for one's country. Do you think that criticism is justified? Write four or five sentences, giving evidence for your views.

Your skills	Possible wording to make use of
Moving from understanding to interpreting	Tennyson's poem celebrates the unthinking heroism of the cavalry … However, his use of …
Examining and exploring **implicit** meaning	The repetition of 'while the world wondered' shows that …
Commenting on what you have discovered	It is all very well for Tennyson to exclaim 'When will their glory fade', but …

GETTING IT INTO WRITING

Comparing poems

Tennyson's poem invites comparison with other poems about war. Later in this cluster you will find 'Kamikaze', 'Poppies', 'Bayonet Charge', 'Exposure', 'Remains' and 'War Photographer'. Another poem which would make a telling comparison would be 'Dulce et Decorum Est' by Wilfred Owen. The title comes from a Latin phrase meaning 'It is sweet and honourable to die for your country' – a sentiment that Owen undermines with his description of men dying horribly from a gas attack.

Choose a poem to compare with 'The Charge of the Light Brigade'. Make notes first (see the following example) and then use the notes to write three or four paragraphs comparing Tennyson's poem with the poem of your choice.

'The Charge of the Light Brigade'

- Regular verse form and rhyme scheme
- The strict beat …
- Uses the language of battle
- The writer is standing back from the action
- The people involved are anonymous
- The poet wants us to celebrate the bravery of the men even though …

GETTING CREATIVE

The Crimean War was one of the first conflicts where newspapers reported on the battles. William Russell of *The Times* broke the story to the public, nearly three weeks after the event.

Using information from the poem, create a news story for a modern newspaper. What headline might a newspaper editor use?

Your response

Do you think a 21st-century attitude to war is generally different from that of someone living in the 19th (or 20th) century? Can you imagine a situation in which it would be possible to believe that it is 'sweet and honourable to die for your country'?

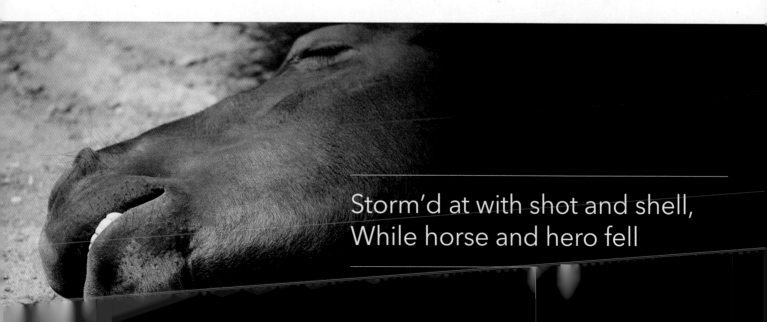

Storm'd at with shot and shell,
While horse and hero fell

CLUSTER 2

Power and conflict
6 Exposure

GETTING STARTED – THE POEM AND YOU

1 Exposure. What does this word mean to you? Work with a partner to jot down the various meanings and contexts that come to mind.

GETTING CLOSER – FOCUS ON DETAILS

First impressions

1 Read the poem. Pick out words that give clues to the time and the place in which it is set.

2 Look at the part the weather plays in the poem. Where can you find references to the weather as if it is an enemy?

Interpreting themes, ideas, attitudes and feelings

1 This is a poem not only about exposure, but also about waiting. Look at the first four verses and pick out any references that you feel indicate a sense of waiting or apprehension.

2 What other feelings does the poem evoke? With a partner discuss these terms and arrange them in order of how appropriate you think they are:

hopelessness	innocence	despair
endurance	suffering	misery
bitterness	survival	fear

EXPOSURE

Our brains ache, in the merciless iced east winds that knive us …
Wearied we keep awake because the night is silent …
Low, drooping flares confuse our memory of the salient …
Worried by silence, sentries whisper, curious, nervous,
　　But nothing happens. 5

Watching, we hear the mad gusts tugging on the wire,
Like twitching agonies of men among its brambles.
Northward, incessantly, the flickering gunnery rumbles,
Far off, like a dull rumour of some other war.
　　What are we doing here? 10

The poignant misery of dawn begins to grow ...
We only know war lasts, rain soaks, and clouds sag stormy.
Dawn massing in the east her melancholy army
Attacks once more in ranks on shivering ranks of grey,
    But nothing happens.   15

Sudden successive flights of bullets streak the silence.
Less deathly than the air that shudders black with snow,
With sidelong flowing flakes that flock, pause and renew;
We watch them wandering up and down the wind's nonchalance,
    But nothing happens.   20

Pale flakes with fingering stealth come feeling for our faces —
We cringe in holes, back on forgotten dreams, and stare, snow-dazed,
Deep into grassier ditches. So we drowse, sun-dozed,
Littered with blossoms trickling where the blackbird fusses,
    — Is it that we are dying?   25

Slowly our ghosts drag home: glimpsing the sunk fires, glozed
With crusted dark-red jewels; crickets jingle there;
For hours the innocent mice rejoice: the house is theirs;
Shutters and doors, all closed: on us the doors are closed, —
    We turn back to our dying.   30

Since we believe not otherwise can kind fires burn;
Nor ever suns smile true on child, or field, or fruit.
For God's invincible spring our love is made afraid;
Therefore, not loath, we lie out here; therefore were born,
    For love of God seems dying.   35

Tonight, this frost will fasten on this mud and us,
Shrivelling many hands, puckering foreheads crisp.
The burying-party, picks and shovels in shaking grasp,
Pause over half-known faces. All their eyes are ice,
    But nothing happens.   40

Wilfred Owen

Listen to the poem on Cambridge Elevate

salient (3): part of a line
of trenches that bulges
out into enemy territory
nonchalance (19):
calmness/relaxation, or
the appearance of it
loath (34): unwilling,
reluctant

PUTTING DETAILS TO USE

Analysing language, form and structure

 1 Work in pairs to read part of the poem closely and make annotations on a copy. Each pair should explore two verses.

Mark the poem with different colours or symbols (underline, circles, wavy lines and so on) to show different features that you notice. These can range from a **?** (need to find out) to ** (this word is interesting). For example:

Slowly our ghosts drag home: glimpsing the sunk fires, glozed

With crusted dark-red jewels; crickets jingle there;

For hours the innocent mice rejoice: the house is theirs;

Shutters and doors, all closed: on us the doors are closed,

We turn back to our dying.

> **?**
>
> Metaphor – dying embers
>
> ** The soldiers?
>
> There is no welcome

 2 As a class, combine the features each pair has noticed. You should now have a grasp, if only in outline, of the whole poem.

✔ Learning checkpoint

One thing you will have noticed is the form the poem takes, with its ABBA rhyme scheme and lines of approximately the same length. In what ways does the poem depart from a conventional form such as this, from John Clare's 'The Landrail':

How sweet and pleasant grows the way

Through summer time again

While landrails call from day to day

Amid the grass and grain

ⓘ Contexts

Wilfred Owen wrote some of the most important poetry of the First World War. His poetry expresses his anger at the cruelty and 'the Pity of War'. This poem comes from Owen's experiences as a soldier on the battle front, in freezing cold conditions. The soldiers appear trapped between life and death. The last verse was written two months before Owen was killed – in the week before the war ended.

Slowly our ghosts drag home: glimpsing the sunk fires, glozed
With crusted dark-red jewels

Show your skills

Write two or three sentences describing the structure (organisation) of Owen's poem and how this affects the way we read it.

Notice the difference between the ways these two examples begin the task:

- *'Exposure' is written in verses of five lines. The lines are roughly the same length apart from …*
- *The unusual length of the lines has the effect of …*

The kernel of the poem

Although we shouldn't view poems as hard nuts to crack, there's no doubt that in some poems there is a 'kernel', a central key area. It's like the crisis in a drama or the 'twist' in many short stories. In 'Exposure', after the image of ghostly soldiers creeping home, comes this verse:

Since we believe not otherwise can kind fires burn;

Nor ever suns smile true on child, or field, or fruit.

For God's invincible spring our love is made afraid;

Therefore, not loath, we lie out here; therefore were born,

For love of God seems dying.

The **syntax** of these lines is hard to unravel. Not surprisingly, people have come up with different interpretations over the years. The majority view seems to be that God's love is absent and that they, the soldiers, are born to die in a sacrifice so that kind fires can burn and that the sun can shine on child, field or fruit. The suggestion is that they are not loath or unwilling to do this – partly perhaps because their actions will have defended their country or partly because in dying their suffering will end.

GETTING IT INTO WRITING

What might be the thoughts and emotions going through the soldiers' minds on this freezing night? Write a diary entry or a letter home from one of the soldiers, using short quotes from the text to support what you say.

Comparing poems

'Exposure' was written by a poet who experienced the things he described. This makes it different from the two preceding poems in this cluster.

What difference does that make to your reading of the poems? Does personal experience help to create a better poem?

Using this difference as your starting point, choose one of the earlier poems in this cluster to compare with 'Exposure'.

GETTING CREATIVE

Here is the first verse with different punctuation and expanded by the insertion of extra words to create a **prose** account. Choose another verse and do the same thing. Try to maintain the tone of the piece as far as possible.

It is so cold that our brains ache. We stand or lean against the parapet in the merciless iced east winds that knive us. Even our greatcoats cannot keep it out. We are wearied but we keep awake because the night is so silent it's unnerving. Low, drooping flares light up No Man's Land and confuse our memory of the salient, which we are guarding. We are worried by the silence and the sentries whisper. They are curious and nervous; will there be a sudden attack – or gas? But nothing happens.

Your response

Think about the idea of No Man's Land. Are these men already in a kind of 'No Man's Land'?

Power and conflict
7 Storm on the Island

GETTING STARTED – THE POEM AND YOU

Read 'Storm on the Island'. There are two strands to this poem – the storm and people's reaction to it. Which strand is, for you, the more important?

GETTING CLOSER – FOCUS ON DETAILS

First impressions

1 What can we deduce about the island? Sketch a plan, diagram or picture of the island from the information provided in the poem.

2 Your response to the previous question will have helped you to realise that much of the poem is about what is not there. Mark a copy of the poem to show where Heaney uses words and phrases that describe things that are absent or negative.

Interpreting themes, ideas, attitudes and feelings

1 What is the response of the people of the island to the weather? Look at these suggestions and arrange them in order from the most appropriate to the least:

practical	not bothered	fearful
resentful	irrational	stoical
vulnerable		

2 The power of nature is a theme in 'Storm on the Island' as it is in the extract from 'The Prelude'. Here, that power is more clearly defined.

Which words and phrases bring out the feeling of nature's power?

 Contexts

Seamus Heaney (1939–2013) was one of the 20th century's most important poets. He was awarded the Nobel Prize for Literature in 1995.

In contrast to his poem 'Follower' in Cluster 1 Unit 10, the theme of this poem is more universal than personal. Like the Romantic poets, Heaney is writing about our relationship with nature, and our vulnerability in the face of its destructive power.

The title, beginning with just 'Storm' rather than 'A storm' or 'The storm', suggests that Heaney is not writing about the experience of a specific storm, but about the power of storms (and nature) in general. The final thought – that what the islanders fear is invisible – gives the poem an almost spiritual dimension.

STORM ON THE ISLAND

We are prepared: we build our houses squat,
Sink walls in rock and roof them with good slate.
This wizened earth has never troubled us
With hay, so, as you see, there are no stacks
Or stooks that can be lost. Nor are there trees   5
Which might prove company when it blows full
Blast: you know what I mean — leaves and branches
Can raise a tragic chorus in a gale
So that you listen to the thing you fear
Forgetting that it pummels your house too.   10
But there are no trees, no natural shelter.
You might think that the sea is company,
Exploding comfortably down on the cliffs,
But no: when it begins, the flung spray hits
The very windows, spits like a tame cat   15
Turned savage. We just sit tight while wind dives
And strafes invisibly. Space is a salvo,
We are bombarded by the empty air.
Strange, it is a huge nothing that we fear.

Seamus Heaney

stooks (5): gathered piles of hay

strafes (17): fires bullets

salvo (17): simultaneous discharge of gunfire

 Listen to the poem on Cambridge Elevate

PUTTING DETAILS TO USE

Analysing language, form and structure

1 The first part of the poem is like the calm before the storm. Where do you first notice words that indicate the coming of the storm?

2 Make a list of the verbs in the last seven lines where the storm really gets underway. What image links most of them? What other comparisons does Heaney use?

3 Take a closer look at Heaney's choice of vocabulary. Here are all the words of the poem in alphabetical order.

a   a   a   a   a   air   and   and   and   are   are   are   are   are   as   be   begins   blast blows   bombarded   branches   build   but   but   by   can   can   cat   chorus   cliffs comfortably   company   company   dives   down   earth   empty   exploding   fear fear   flung   forgetting   full   gale   good   had   has   hay   hits   house   houses huge   I   in   in   invisibly   is   is   is   it   it   it   it   just   know   leaves   like   listen lost   mean   might   might   natural   never   no   no   no   no   nor   nothing   on or   our   prepared   prove   pummels   raise   rock   roof   salvo   savage   sea   see shelter   sink   sit   slate   so   so   space   spits   spray   squat   stacks   stooks   strafes strange   tame   that   that   that   that   that   the   the   the   the   the   the   the   them there   there   there   thing   think   this   tight   to   too   tragic   trees   trees   troubled turned   us   very   walls   we   we   we   we   we   what   when   when   which   while wind   windows   with   with   wizened   you   you   you   you   you   your

You will notice that there are many repetitions. Pick three examples of repetition and say why they are of interest. For example:

can	Used twice in the first part of the poem. This is what might happen or has happened in the past. Later in the poem it's as if it is actually happening.
company	
fear	
you/your	
we	
no	

4 How many syllables does each line have? Is the pattern regular? If you compare the way it is written to the extract from 'The Prelude', what differences do you notice?

✓ **Learning checkpoint**

Write a few sentences (about 100 words) to give your views on the following:

- Who is speaking in the poem and what do we know about him or her?
- Who might they be speaking to?
- What is their attitude to the island?
- What is their attitude to the storms?

Show your skills

Now look at these answers and assess how successfully they answer the questions, give their reasons and go beyond stating what is explicit to 'reading between the lines'.

The speaker is Seamus Heaney because he wrote the poem and he is living on the island. He must be speaking to a visitor who does not know about the island. His attitude to the island is that it is his home but it is not very comfortable and it doesn't have fields of hay or trees. He does not like the storm because he says he is fearful of it.

The speaker sounds as if he has been on the island a long time. 'We build our houses squat' suggests knowledge over many years as house building would not take place very often. The person he is speaking to obviously doesn't know all this so must be a stranger. The speaker feels they have made the best of a bad situation in resisting the elements. When the storm comes they just 'sit tight' and wait for it to be over so although it can be frightening it is something they are used to – a bit like living through the Blitz during the war.

The speaker sounds male because of all the imagery of war. He has lived on the island a long time – 'has never troubled us' implies a long stretch of time. Here he seems to be speaking to a visitor as he says 'as you see'. You can't quite tell how he feels about the island. He description makes it sound barren and isolated and yet there is a feeling of pride in surviving the worst that storms can throw at them.

the flung spray hits
The very windows, spits like a tame cat
Turned savage.

GETTING IT INTO WRITING

As you have already explored, 'Storm on the Island' is unusual in being as much about absences as it is about things that are present. See, for example, Heaney's use of **irony** when he writes 'The wizened earth has never troubled us / With hay'. Write a paragraph or two (100–150 words) explaining the things that are missing and how this affects the people on the island. You could start by making rough notes like this:

Absence	Effect on the islanders
No hay	Probably not much livestock
No trees	Not much shelter; also …

Comparing poems

In this activity you will prepare a comparison of this poem with two other poems, the extract from 'The Prelude' and 'Ozymandias'. Here is a partly completed table to get you started. Leave space after each note you make.

'Storm on the Island'	'The Prelude'	'Ozymandias'
		Sonnet form
	Personal recollection	
Conversational tone		
	Little use of comparisons (**similes**/**metaphors**)	
		Has a clear message
Present tense		
Sounds and the lack of them are important		

Having made a table of rough notes, look at each one and ask: **Why?** Try to answer that question in the space you have left. For example:

Present tense – gives a sense of drama – and implies storms are constantly occurring.		

Your response

Is the island the sort of place you would want to visit - or to live? What would make people want to go there, or want to remain there?

Explore the poem further with a video activity on Cambridge Elevate

Power and conflict
8 Bayonet Charge

GETTING STARTED – THE POEM AND YOU

1 Use words from the following collection to create four or five titles or headlines, such as: 'THE DIGNITY OF DYNAMITE', 'SWEATING MAN DAZZLED WITH STARS' or 'SILENT TERROR OF BEWILDERMENT'.

> a across air alarm almost and arm as awoke bayonet belly between bewilderment blue brimmed bullets centre chest circle clockwork clods cold crackling crawled dark dazzled dignity dropped dynamite etcetera eye eyes field fire flame foot footfalls for from furrows get green had hand hare has he hearing heavy hedge his honour hot human hung in iron its jumped khaki king like listening lugged luxuries man mid-stride molten mouth nations numb of open out past patriotic plunged pointing raw raw-seamed reason rifle rolled running runs second shot-slashed silent smacking smashed standing stars statuary still stopped stumbling suddenly sweat sweating tear terror's that the then threshing threw to touchy toward towards up was what who wide with yelling yellow

2 Share what you have written in a small group and select one title/headline from each person to share with the class.

   a What kinds of images are you able to convey with the words in the poem?

   b Are there any strong themes that you notice in the words that Hughes has chosen to use?

3 Now read or listen to 'Bayonet Charge'.

 Contexts

British poet Ted Hughes (1930–1998) became Poet Laureate in 1984, and is thought of as one of the best English poets of the last century.

Unlike the experience described by Owen in 'Exposure', running across a field towards enemy guns, carrying a weapon to shoot and stab people was not something Hughes had done. He was, though, fascinated by his father's stories of fighting in the First World War. Hughes only had stories and imagination to go on, together perhaps with some photos or archive films.

BAYONET CHARGE

Suddenly he awoke and was running — raw
In raw-seamed hot khaki, his sweat heavy,
Stumbling across a field of clods towards a green hedge
That dazzled with rifle fire, hearing
Bullets smacking the belly out of the air —   5
He lugged a rifle numb as a smashed arm;
The patriotic tear that had brimmed in his eye
Sweating like molten iron from the centre of his chest, —

In bewilderment then he almost stopped —
In what cold clockwork of the stars and the nations   10
Was he the hand pointing that second? He was running
Like a man who has jumped up in the dark and runs
Listening between his footfalls for the reason
Of his still running, and his foot hung like
Statuary in mid-stride. Then the shot-slashed furrows   15

Threw up a yellow hare that rolled like a flame
And crawled in a threshing circle, its mouth wide
Open silent, its eyes standing out.
He plunged past with his bayonet toward the green hedge.
King, honour, human dignity, etcetera   20
Dropped like luxuries in a yelling alarm
To get out of that blue crackling air
His terror's touchy dynamite.

Ted Hughes

 Listen to the poem on Cambridge Elevate

GETTING CLOSER – FOCUS ON DETAILS

First impressions

1 Look at these brief descriptions. Put three of them together in a way that you think best sums up the poem. You could replace 'he' with 'a soldier' in any of the sentences.

a   He almost forgets why he is running.
b   He feels terrified but he manages to carry on.
c   He is bewildered and almost stops.
d   He is hot and sweaty.
e   He is running towards the enemy lines as part of an attack.
f   He no longer feels patriotic.
g   He runs across No Man's Land towards the enemy trenches.
h   He rushes on, desperate to get out of the bullets.
i   He wonders why he is doing it.

2 Does it surprise you that Hughes did not have direct experience of a bayonet charge such as the one described in the poem?

Pick out words or phrases that you think bring the experience to life for the reader.

Interpreting themes, ideas, attitudes and feelings

In this poem, Hughes tries to do two things: to describe the physical experience of the bayonet charge and to explore the mental experience. It is as if it is the mental experience that interests him, but he cannot convey it to a reader without communicating the physical experience first.

Make a table, or two columns, to distinguish between the two aspects of the poem. For example the fact that the soldier is running and that his uniform feels heavy would come under 'physical' but the fact that a 'patriotic tear ... had brimmed in his eye' would come under 'mental'.

PUTTING DETAILS TO USE

Analysing language, form and structure

1 Hughes's language is known for its vigour and its directness. Use a copy of the poem to highlight only the verbs (yellow) and the nouns (green). For example:

> Suddenly he awoke and was running – raw
> In raw-seamed hot khaki, his sweat heavy,
> Stumbling across a field of clods towards a
>   green hedge
> That dazzled with rifle fire, hearing
> Bullets smacking the belly out of the air –

2 See if you can group the words you have highlighted into clusters with related meanings. For example you could put 'hare', 'green', 'hedge', 'furrows' into a group.

3 There are far fewer adjectives, though they are also revealing. Highlight them in a different colour and see what kinds of adjectives Hughes has chosen.

PSI (poetry scene investigation)

Use the table below to explore some of the more interesting aspects of the poem:

Evidence	Questions
'Suddenly he awoke and was running – raw'	He awoke – from what? A trance?
'In raw-seamed hot khaki, his sweat heavy,'	Why 'raw'? A 'raw recruit'? Tender?
'etcetera'	
'cold clockwork of the stars'	
'Threw up a yellow hare'	Is this real? If not, what does it signify?
'His terror's touchy dynamite.'	Terror like dynamite? Might explode?

Learning checkpoint

Hughes does not mention anything about being frightened until the last line. Write two or three sentences to explain how Hughes manages to express feelings of fear or terror without using those words. You could also think about the way the lines are punctuated, which affects their rhythm and the way you read them – especially if you do so aloud.

GETTING IT INTO WRITING

Show your skills

What do you now understand about the poem and what you can **infer**? Write a paragraph or two (about 200 words) explaining what you think Hughes is trying to achieve in the poem and how he tries to do it. You can also speculate on why he does it. You might want to use some of the following phrases:

He is trying to communicate the feeling of …

Hughes wants to get inside the …

The poet is imagining what it must be like …

In particular he is interested in how …

He shows this in the way that …

Interestingly, mid-way through …

He manages to convey … by/through …

I think that …

On the other hand …

Comparing poems

Here is an extract from Wilfred Owen's poem 'Spring Offensive' which could be compared to some lines from 'Bayonet Charge':

So, soon they topped the hill, and raced together
Over an open stretch of herb and heather
Exposed. And instantly the whole sky burned
With fury against them; earth set sudden cups
In thousands for their blood;

Compare these lines with the first verse of Hughes's poem. Write a paragraph to say what you think they have in common and in what ways they differ.

Your response

1 Does 'Bayonet Charge' have any relevance to you – or is it just like watching a film or doing a history project? Discuss your ideas with a partner.

2 Have you ever felt intense fear? Was it anything like the experience Hughes describes – for instance with the sensation of time stopping or slowing down?

In what cold clockwork of the stars and the nations
Was he the hand pointing that second?

Power and conflict
9 Remains

GETTING STARTED – THE POEM AND YOU

Read 'Remains'. This poem comes from a collection by Simon Armitage called
The Not Dead. Why do you think that title was chosen?

Contexts

Simon Armitage was born in Yorkshire in 1963.

The material for his poetry collection *The Not Dead* comes from interviews with ex-soldiers, which were part of a Channel 4 film with the same title. Armitage's role was to listen to the soldiers' stories and turn them into poems. In his introduction to the collection he says that for a lot of the soldiers, being in the film meant that they had to relive terrible experiences. To capture this feeling, many of the poems in the collection revolve around a 'flashback' of a bad memory.

GETTING CLOSER – FOCUS ON DETAILS

First impressions

1 The poem's title is 'Remains'. What meanings can that word have?

2 With a partner, come up with an alternative title for the poem. Share your ideas with the class.

Interpreting themes, ideas, attitudes and feelings

1 In pairs or small groups, decide which of these terms are the most appropriate to describe the feelings of the soldier now. You may swap some words for those of your own if you wish. Arrange the words in a diamond shape with the most suitable at the top:

> fear   guilt   horror   resentment   disgust   shock   remorse   depression   helplessness

2 For each of the three words at the top of your diamond, find a phrase in the poem to provide evidence for it.

REMAINS

Listen to the poem on Cambridge Elevate

On another occasion, we get sent out
to tackle looters raiding a bank.
And one of them legs it up the road,
probably armed, possibly not.

Well myself and somebody else and somebody else   5
are all of the same mind,
so all three of us open fire.
Three of a kind all letting fly, and I swear

I see every round as it rips through his life –
I see broad daylight on the other side.   10
So we've hit this looter a dozen times
and he's there on the ground, sort of inside out.

pain itself, the image of agony.
One of my mates goes by
and tosses his guts back into his body.   15
Then he's carted off in the back of a lorry.

End of story, except not really.
His blood-shadow stays on the street, and out on patrol
I walk right over it week after week.
Then I'm home on leave. But I blink   20

and he bursts again through the doors of the bank.
Sleep, and he's probably armed, possibly not.
Dream, and he's torn apart by a dozen rounds.
And the drink and the drugs won't flush him out –

he's here in my head when I close my eyes,   25
dug in between enemy lines,
not left for dead in some distant, sun-stunned, sand-smothered land
or six-feet-under in desert sand,

but near to the knuckle, here and now,
his bloody life in my bloody hands.   30

Simon Armitage

PUTTING DETAILS TO USE

Analysing language, form and structure

1 The poem is noticeable for its use of down-to-earth language as it was spoken (or could well have been spoken) by the soldier. Read the poem again and mark where it is as if the words are spoken, not written, for example 'legs it'.

2 Towards the end of the poem there is the use of 'sun-stunned, sand-smothered' and other phrases that you would not expect in everyday speech. Mark these too. Is this change of style sudden or gradual as the poem progresses?

3 Compare your findings as a class. What inferences can you make?

4 Do you think this works as a poem – or would it be better in a different form? What other form could it be written in?

Show your skills

In which of the following statements has the student moved from **describing** or **explaining** to **analysing** or **exploring** in discussing the nature of conflict in the poem?

A The real conflict lies in the mind of the soldier and it is not just present as a memory he would rather forget but as something embedded within him. The memory has 'dug in' and will not be 'flushed out', so that his conflicted emotions will always be inside his head.

B In the first part of the poem, the soldier is describing the incident where the looter was shot and in the second part he describes how this has affected the soldier ever since. In the first part the conflict is in the streets but in the second part it is within the soldier's mind.

C The 'remains' of the dead man are not just his body but firstly the blood-shadow on the pavement like an indelible mark and later still the image that remains in his mind. That image and the emotions it evokes have dug into the soldier's consciousness and cannot be erased. It is behind enemy lines – but who is the enemy now?

 Learning checkpoint

The poem is written using a lot of the phrases the soldier would have used. However, by the end, you are aware that these are Armitage's words, or his arrangement of other people's words. What gives that impression? Write four or five sentences to explain how you can deduce that this is a crafted piece of writing rather than the words of a soldier, verbatim (i.e. as he spoke them)? You might want to make use of the following phrases:

At the beginning of the poem, the writer uses …

Towards the end of the poem, the language …

Some examples of repetition show that …

There are some typical poetic devices. such as …

All of these examples show that …

near to the knuckle, here and now,
his bloody life in my bloody hands.

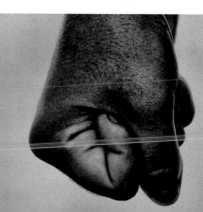

GETTING IT INTO WRITING

Look closer at language choices by considering the following phrases and where they occur in the poem. Now write a couple of paragraphs exploring why you think the writer has chosen these words and not some of the obvious alternatives:

* 'legs it up the road' (rather than 'runs away')
* 'myself and somebody else and somebody else' (rather than 'and the other men' or men's names)
* 'all letting fly' (rather than 'shooting')
* 'tosses his guts' (rather than 'rearranges the body')
* 'carted off' (rather than 'taken away')
* 'torn apart' (rather than 'hit by').

Comparing poems

Looking back at the other poems in this cluster, which do you think would make the best comparison? You might be looking for another poem that includes a death – or one that involves guilt or shame. Perhaps you would be looking for other **first-person narratives** or those that recount a first-hand experience.

Choose two poems and jot down the reasons why you think these would be good poems to compare 'Remains' with. A class discussion will show how far others agree with you.

GETTING CREATIVE

Take the words of the poem and use them as part of a play-script or a film-script. Invent one or more other characters and give them some additional lines to speak. For example:

Soldier: Then he's carted off in the back of a lorry.
Soldier's brother (for example): Was that it? My God! What happened next?
Soldier: End of story, except not really.
Soldier's brother: What do you mean? Was there an inquiry?
Soldier: Nothing like that. It's just that his blood-shadow …

Your response

In his introduction to *The Not Dead*, Simon Armitage says that many of the soldiers he spoke to had always known that they wanted to go to battle, but they weren't prepared for what they would feel like when they came home. The speaker in 'Remains' lists some of the ways he has tried to deal with his memories, but also that they haven't worked. Do you think he would have been more able to cope with what he saw if he had been better prepared, or do you think he (and others like him) would always have struggled with a memory like this?

Power and conflict
10 Poppies

IN REMEMBRANCE

GETTING STARTED – THE POEM AND YOU

What are your feelings when a parent or carer checks how you look before you go out? Do you wait stoically for it to be over/squirm impatiently/rush off as soon as you can? Do you return farewells affectionately/grumpily/not at all?

GETTING CLOSER – FOCUS ON DETAILS

First impressions

Read 'Poppies'. Then discuss these questions with a partner:

a   At the beginning of the poem, a mother remembers seeing her child off to school. Son or daughter? – what gives you a clue?

b   We can work out the date. What is it?

c   It is not the child's first day at school, so why do you think the mother seems emotional?

The first two questions can be answered from explicit evidence in the poem. The last relies on what you can infer and using your imagination.

Interpreting themes, ideas, attitudes and feelings

The narrator seems to move from one time and place to another in this poem. **Symbols** and actions associated with peace and normal domestic life are interspersed with those that refer back to war and conflict.

1 Make a list of all the references to time you can find, starting with 'Three days before Armistice Sunday' and 'Before you left' – you should be able to find at least five clues.

2 Make two lists, one of references to peace and normality (for example 'Sellotape', 'white cat hairs') and one of references to conflict (for example 'Armistice', 'poppies').

3 Where is the narrator? Does her location help to explain why the memory of her child leaving is mixed in with such vivid and fearful imagery? Look carefully at the last verse and you may be able to 'place' her.

ℹ Contexts

Jane Weir was born in Italy in 1963, and grew up in Italy and Manchester. She also lived in Northern Ireland during the 1980s. 'Poppies' was written in response to the losses suffered during the wars in Iraq and Afghanistan. Armistice Sunday started in 1918 as a way of marking the end of the First World War (an 'armistice' is an agreement to stop fighting), and now shares the date with Remembrance Day, which is a way to commemorate soldiers lost in all wars. Around the world, poppies are worn and laid at memorials, inspired by the poppies which grew over the graves of fallen soldiers.

POPPIES

Three days before Armistice Sunday
and poppies had already been placed
on individual war graves. Before you left,
I pinned one onto your lapel, crimped petals,
spasms of paper red, disrupting a blockade   5
of yellow bias binding around your blazer.

Sellotape bandaged around my hand,
I rounded up as many white cat hairs
as I could, smoothed down your shirt's
upturned collar, steeled the softening   10
of my face. I wanted to graze my nose
across the tip of your nose, play at
being Eskimos like we did when
you were little. I resisted the impulse
to run my fingers through the gelled   15
blackthorns of your hair. All my words
flattened, rolled, turned into felt,

slowly melting. I was brave, as I walked
with you, to the front door, threw
it open, the world overflowing
like a treasure chest. A split second
and you were away, intoxicated.
After you'd gone I went into your bedroom,
released a song bird from its cage.
Later a single dove flew from the pear tree,
and this is where it has led me,
skirting the church yard walls, my stomach busy
making tucks, darts, pleats, hat-less, without
a winter coat or reinforcements of scarf, gloves.

On reaching the top of the hill I traced
the inscriptions on the war memorial,
leaned against it like a wishbone.
The dove pulled freely against the sky,
an ornamental stitch. I listened, hoping to hear
your playground voice catching on the wind.

Jane Weir

bias binding (6): strip of
fabric used for edging
clothes

PUTTING DETAILS TO USE

Analysing language, form and structure

1 Write the poem out as prose (with no line endings). Then try inserting the line endings to see how close your version is to the original (don't peep, it will be interesting to see if you decide differently to the writer).

2 Read your new version of the text aloud. Is it still a poem or has it become a piece of autobiographical prose, like a personal diary entry?

Show your skills

Look more closely at Weir's use of language. Choose three or four examples that you find interesting, and comment on the selections you have made. For example:

'spasms of paper red'	'Spasms' of red paper is an unusual description – it suggests jagged movement as if the paper hasn't been cut properly. It's odd and it doesn't create a good image for me. Why paper red, not red paper?
'leaned against it like a wishbone'	She was bent over. Though a wishbone suggests she was bent double as if in pain. Perhaps she was also making a wish for her son's safety.

You can see that there is room for speculation and for opinion. 'It's odd and it doesn't create a good image for me' is a fair comment, but needs a little more explanation. Why doesn't it create a good image? For example: '… because Remembrance poppies are not jagged, but made up of smooth curves.' Remember to consider **why** the poet might have made an unusual choice – if poppies are usually smooth, is the word 'spasms' important for another reason?

GETTING IT INTO WRITING

This poet is also a textile artist. How is her interest in fabrics revealed in her writing? Write three or four sentences to answer this question. Be ready to comment on what you discover as well as to describe it. In this way you will be showing that you can explore as well as describe and explain.

Learning checkpoint

The form of the poem may be free verse (poetry that is 'free' from the restrictions of rhyme and rhythm), but the language is not that of ordinary speech.

Look at the first verse and pick out where the language seems more intense, more carefully arranged, than everyday speech or writing.

Comparing poems

Which poem from this cluster would work well as a comparison with 'Poppies'? As it was written by a **contemporary** poet in response to modern conflicts, perhaps a good starting point might be 'Remains'. Or, as the imagery is of the First World War, you could may want to consider 'Exposure' or 'Bayonet Charge' as a comparison. You could also compare a poem that combines a scene of everyday life with language that relates to war and conflict, such as 'Storm on the Island'.

Alternatively, and to gain practice for the 'Unseen poetry' section of your exam, you could look at Cecil Day-Lewis's 'Walking Away' (see Cluster 1 Unit 7), which you will see has similarities with 'Poppies'.

Your response

Is this a poem about war? Is it a poem about conflict – and if so, what is the conflict between?

Explore the poem further with a video activity on Cambridge Elevate

Power and conflict
11 War Photographer

GETTING STARTED – THE POEM AND YOU

Newspapers carry photographs and television news broadcasts show clips from war zones. Which of these statements do you agree with? (You may well agree with more than one.)

a   I try not to look at them.
b   They may be horrible but they are fascinating.
c   I look at them and then think of something else.
d   They remind me how safe I am.
e   The suffering I see is bad, but I can't do anything about it.
f   They make me angry.

GETTING CLOSER – FOCUS ON DETAILS

First impressions

1 Read 'War Photographer'. The poem is a portrait of a reporter whose job it is to capture images of conflict. The poem was written several years ago, before digital photography. How do you know this?

2 Where in the poem does the image the photographer is developing start to become clear?

Contexts

This poem is by Carol Ann Duffy – the first woman (and the first person from Scotland) to be British Poet Laureate, which she has been since 2009.

Before digital photography, developing and printing photos was a time-consuming and skilled process. Most people took their film to a shop to be developed and printed. For the professional photographer, like the one in the poem, it was important to develop and print your own photographs so that you could control how they looked. The most important stage in the process is when the image begins to appear on the developing paper in the tray that holds the developing liquid. On the plain white sheet, darker forms start to appear until, gradually, the image becomes clear.

WAR PHOTOGRAPHER

In his darkroom he is finally alone
with spools of suffering set out in ordered rows.
The only light is red and softly glows,
as though this were a church and he
a priest preparing to intone a Mass.   5
Belfast. Beirut. Phnom Penh. All flesh is grass.

He has a job to do. Solutions slop in trays
beneath his hands, which did not tremble then
though seem to now. Rural England. Home again
to ordinary pain which simple weather can dispel,   10
to fields which don't explode beneath the feet
of running children in a nightmare heat.

Something is happening. A stranger's features
faintly start to twist before his eyes,
a half-formed ghost. He remembers the cries   15
of this man's wife, how he sought approval
without words to do what someone must
and how the blood stained into foreign dust.

A hundred agonies in black and white
from which his editor will pick out five or six   20
for Sunday's supplement. The reader's eyeballs prick
with tears between the bath and pre-lunch beers.
From the aeroplane he stares impassively at where
he earns his living and they do not care.

Carol Ann Duffy

 Listen to the poem on Cambridge Elevate

Interpreting themes, ideas, attitudes and feelings

1 Work with a partner to write a summary of each verse. Make notes of any feelings or ideas evoked by the verse. Also jot down any words or phrases that you think need further investigation. These might be phrases that you're not sure about or ones that seem to carry an important meaning. For example:

Poem	Summary	Comment
In his darkroom he is finally alone with spools of suffering set out in ordered rows. The only light is red and softly glows, as though this were a church and he a priest preparing to intone a Mass. Belfast. Beirut. Phnom Penh. All flesh is grass.	The photographer develops his pictures in his darkroom. Places of conflict are mentioned. 'All flesh is grass' is a quote from the Bible meaning 'life is fragile'.	Everything is quiet and orderly as if taking place in church. The last line is a sharp contrast, reminding us what the photos are about.

2 As a class, combine ideas and see if there are any areas of disagreement or of particular interest.

Learning checkpoint

What impression do you get of the photographer's feelings? Write two or three sentences to describe them, using key words from the poem to guide you.

Show your skills

Look at the following extracts from students who have been asked to write about the last two lines of the poem. Use different highlighters on a copy of the extracts to mark:

a where the writer shows understanding
b where the writer explores the text further, perhaps 'reading between the lines'
c where the writer has given a personal interpretation or response.

The photographer is travelling to another assignment and looking down at the place where he will be taking photos. He is impassive, which means not showing any emotion. The final words, 'they do not care', refer to the people who look at his photos.

The photographer is looking down at 'where he earns a living' which could be a war-torn country or it could be England, where they pay him. Either way, it seems likely that 'they' who don't care must be the newspaper readers – though he can't know that.

He is impassive, which implies that he doesn't care but we know from earlier in the poem that he remembers one incident vividly and trembles. From an aeroplane he can look down on the places where he earns a living and it also seems like he's looking down on us, the people who read the newspapers.

PUTTING DETAILS TO USE

Analysing language, form and structure

1 The poet has chosen a simple verse form with a mostly regular rhyming pattern. At one point the poet chooses to use **assonance** rather than conventional rhyme – where does this happen?

2 The regularity of the form is disturbed by the many short staccato sentences in between smooth run-on lines. Take a copy of the poem and highlight or underline each individual 'sentence' to see this for yourself.

3 This irregularity within the surface regularity creates a disturbing contrast. In fact, much of the poem's force depends on using contrast. How many examples can you find where the poet presents two contrasting or opposing images or feelings? This is a starting point:

'he is finally alone'	
'his hands which did not tremble then'	'though seem to now.'
'Belfast. Beirut. Phnom Penh.'	

GETTING IT INTO WRITING

You are now ready to write a short piece about the poem as a whole in response to the question: **How does the poet manage to convey her feelings about war?**

Remember, when you write about a poem, show your skills in:

- including details of what happens
- using individual words in any quotations to support your comments
- exploring implied meaning
- looking for different **perspectives**.

Comparing poems

A number of units in this cluster explore the theme of war – as well as other types of conflict. Look out for the ways that the writers tackle the theme and how the poems (directly or indirectly) convey their attitudes.

Your response

How far do you sympathise with the war photographer? What do you think of the character of the editor? On what basis is the editor choosing the pictures?

Power and conflict
12 Tissue

GETTING STARTED – THE POEM AND YOU

1 What does the word 'tissue' conjure up for you? What associations does it have? Jot down as many associations as you can think of in one minute and then compare them with those of a partner.

2 Make a composite list as a class, using a whiteboard and putting the most common associations in the middle and more unusual ones towards the edge. Later, you can return to this diagram and see how far it matches your impressions of the poem.

GETTING CLOSER – FOCUS ON DETAILS

First impressions

1 Read through the poem, then pause. Now read it again. Close the book and jot down any words or phrases you remember.

2 Once again, compare these with someone else's list and combine the two. Choose one word and write it in large letters on a sheet of A4 paper. When everyone is ready, hold up your word. Discuss, as a class, why these words are memorable or significant.

Interpreting themes, ideas, attitudes and feelings

This is quite a mysterious poem. Like the material we call tissue, the poem seems light and insubstantial. However, there is a conflict within the poem (and perhaps, though we can never be sure) within the poet. Arrange these statements in order according to how well you think they fit the poem:

a It concerns what is real and what is imaginary.

b The poem sets a solid world against a transparent one.

c The writer desires a different, freer, lighter world.

d The writer admires things that are beautiful but not permanent.

e The poem is a dream.

f There is a conflict in the writer's mind beneath a calm surface.

 Contexts

The writer of this poem, Imtiaz Dharker, is a Scottish poet, artist and film-maker. She was born in Pakistan and her family moved to Glasgow in the 1950s, when she was still a baby. Her background and experience of different cultures provide the themes for her poetry: cultural identity, exile, travel, freedom and conflict.

 Listen to the poem on Cambridge Elevate

TISSUE

Paper that lets the light
shine through, this
is what could alter things.
Paper thinned by age or touching,

the kind you find in well-used books,   5
the back of the Koran, where a hand
has written in the names and histories,
who was born to whom,

the height and weight, who
died where and how, on which sepia date, 10
pages smoothed and stroked and turned
transparent with attention.

If buildings were paper, I might
feel their drift, see how easily
they fall away on a sigh, a shift   15
in the direction of the wind.

Maps too. The sun shines through
their borderlines, the marks
that rivers make, roads,
railtracks, mountainfolds,   20

Fine slips from grocery shops
that say how much was sold
and what was paid by credit card
might fly our lives like paper kites.

An architect could use all this,   25
place layer over layer, luminous
script over numbers over line,
and never wish to build again with brick

or block, but let the daylight break
through capitals and monoliths,   30
through the shapes that pride can make,
find a way to trace a grand design

with living tissue, raise a structure
never meant to last,
of paper smoothed and stroked   35
and thinned to be transparent,

turned into your skin.

Imtiaz Dharker

PUTTING DETAILS TO USE

Analysing language, form and structure

1 Look more carefully at the nouns from the poem. (Notice that although 'tissue' is the title, the word 'paper' occurs six times.) Sort them into the categories 'heavy' and 'light'. You may wish to have a third category – 'not sure' – but try not to use that one too much. For example:

Heavy	Light	Not sure
block	paper	

Some of your decisions will be straightforward, but there may be others that are not so easy. For example is 'names' or 'date' light or heavy in Dharker's poem?

2 The poem is written in free verse but divided into verses of four lines, no line being longer than eight words. Given the text displayed as continuous prose, where would you insert line endings and verse breaks?

Paper that lets the light shine through, this is what could alter things. Paper thinned by age or touching, the kind you find in well-used books, the back of the Koran, where a hand has written in the names and histories, who was born to whom, the height and weight, who died where and how, on which sepia date, pages smoothed and stroked and turned transparent with attention. If buildings were paper, I might feel their drift, see how easily they fall away on a sigh, a shift in the direction of the wind. Maps too. The sun shines through their borderlines, the marks that rivers make, roads, railtracks, mountainfolds, fine slips from grocery shops that say how much was sold and what was paid by credit card might fly our lives like paper kites. An architect could use all this, place layer over layer, luminous script over numbers over line, and never wish to build again with brick or block, but let the daylight break through capitals and monoliths, through the shapes that pride can make, find a way to trace a grand design with living tissue, raise a structure never meant to last, of paper smoothed and stroked and thinned to be transparent, turned into your skin.

Learning checkpoint

Write a few sentences (about 100 words), to explain how the poem changes as it develops. You might begin: 'The poem begins with a description of the kind of paper that tends to be found in …' Another sentence might start: 'However, in verses four and five …'

Show your skills

The poem is full of visual contrasts and contradictions: buildings made of paper, kites made from credit-card slips, for example. How well do these statements sum up this aspect of the poem? Put them in a rank order from best to worst and jot down your reasons why. Look out for instances where the writer goes further than explanation and explores the poem or offers a personal response that is justified by the text.

A I get the feeling that the writer would like to live in a world that was not controlled by banks ('paid by credit card') and borders – maps, roads and rivers being symbols of borders.

B The poet contrasts the lightness of paper with the heaviness of bricks and blocks yet I am sure she would not want to live in a paper house.

C Our lives tend to be measured by where we were born, the money we spend and the places we live in. Other things, which might be less substantial, can be more important.

D An architect could be God or nature, creating living tissue out of lifeless material – 'paper smoothed and stroked' but which – being alive – will not be a structure that will last a long time.

GETTING IT INTO WRITING

Comparing poems

Look back over the poems you have read in this cluster and select one that you feel also contains a sense of inner conflict. For example you might want to consider the extract from 'The Prelude', 'Remains' or 'War Photographer'. Compare your chosen poem with 'Tissue' and try to ensure that you cover the following:

Themes – this is what the poem seems to be about, the attitude of the poet (or the character the poet creates) and also the tone or mood, which you can pick up from the way the theme is communicated.

Form and **structure** – how the poem is put together. This includes how it looks on the page and the way the writer treats an existing form such as sonnet or blank verse. This will inevitably include a mention of rhythm and rhyme, or the lack of it.

Language – which might include words and phrases you find particularly striking or significant, the use of imagery or personification and other poetic devices such as alliteration. But you should only write about these aspects if you can see why they are significant.

Finally, give an **opinion**!

Your response

1 Is it essential to understand everything about a poem (or a song, painting and so on) in order to respond to it? Why, or why not?

2 If you were asked to illustrate this poem, what images would you use?

and what was paid by credit card might fly our lives like paper kites.

Power and conflict
13 The Emigrée

GETTING STARTED - THE POEM AND YOU

In this poem, the writer is recalling a place she left many years ago. She does not remember details, but the place has left a very strong impression.

Think back nine or ten years and see if you can recall a place from that time – perhaps somewhere you visited or somewhere you used to live.

a   What memories do you have about the place?
b   What feelings do you associate with it?

GETTING CLOSER - FOCUS ON DETAILS

First impressions

Read the poem. Then, with a partner, look at the following statements about the person in the poem and sort them into the following categories: 'Things I am fairly sure of/things that might be true' or 'Things that I'm fairly sure are not true':

a   As time passes, the impression of sunlight grows stronger.
b   Her home country is not a democracy.
c   Her strongest memory of her city is sunlight.
d   She has no hope of going back.
e   She is a refugee from a war zone.
f   She now lives in a different city.
g   She remembers something of the language of her city.
h   She was very young when she left her home.
i   She would like to go back to her city.
j   The city in which she now lives is not friendly.

> ### ⓘ Contexts
>
> Carol Rumens was born in London in 1944, and has published many collections of her poems. You can see how she plays with the positive and negative throughout this poem. Some clues about why she has done this can perhaps be seen in what she has said about herself and her writing. Rather than calling herself a poet, she would rather be known as 'someone who loves language, and who tries to make various things with it'.

THE EMIGREE

There once was a country… I left it as a child
but my memory of it is sunlight-clear
for it seems I never saw it in that November
which, I am told, comes to the mildest city.
The worst news I receive of it cannot break   5
my original view, the bright, filled paperweight.
It may be at war, it may be sick with tyrants,
but I am branded by an impression of sunlight.

The white streets of that city, the graceful slopes
glow even clearer as time rolls its tanks   10
and the frontiers rise between us, close like waves.
That child's vocabulary I carried here
like a hollow doll, opens and spills a grammar.
Soon I shall have every coloured molecule of it.
It may by now be a lie, banned by the state   15
but I can't get it off my tongue. It tastes of sunlight.

I have no passport, there's no way back at all
but my city comes to me in its own white plane.
It lies down in front of me, docile as paper;
I comb its hair and love its shining eyes.   20
My city takes me dancing through the city
of walls. They accuse me of absence, they circle me.
They accuse me of being dark in their free city.
My city hides behind me. They mutter death,
and my shadow falls as evidence of sunlight.   25

Carol Rumens

 Listen to the poem on Cambridge Elevate

Interpreting themes, ideas, attitudes and feelings

The poem communicates a kaleidoscope of feelings rather than telling a story or describing a place. These feelings are often mixed as you can see from looking at any section of the poem.

1 Using two different colours on a copy of the text, take a section (a verse or part of a verse) and mark positive aspects and negative aspects. Add comments where you think it helps to explain why something is positive or negative. For example:

Positive		Negative
Sounds like the beginning of a fairy tale	There once was a country… I left it as a child	But she left it
She has a strong sunny memory	but my memory of it is sunlight-clear	
	for it seems I never saw it in that November	November is usually seen as a dreary month
	which, I am told, comes to the mildest city.	
Even bad news cannot change her view	The worst news I receive of it cannot break	Bad news
	my original view, the bright, filled paperweight.	
In spite of everything, she retains the sunny memory	It may be at war, it may be sick with tyrants,	War, tyranny
	but I am branded by an impression of sunlight.	Branding is painful, sign of a captive animal

You can see that the conflict that the writer feels is shown in each verse, almost within each line. You can notice it in a simple word like the repeated use of 'but'.

2 What do you think is the nature of the conflict the writer is feeling? Pair up these possible answers and then arrange them in order of importance.

a	The past		f	How she remembers the city
b	Memory and imagination		g	The city she lives in now
c	The news from the city she once knew	versus	h	Darkness and shadows in the new city
d	The sunlight of the old city		i	Reality
e	The city she once knew		j	The present

PUTTING DETAILS TO USE

Analysing language, form and structure

The poem is distinguished from prose by its division into lines of roughly the same length (whether of words or stressed syllables) and into verses of the same length.

In what other ways is it different to a piece of prose writing?

1 To help you answer, look at the following extract and then read it aloud:

My city takes me dancing through the city
of walls. They accuse me of absence, they
   circle me.
They accuse me of being dark in their free
   city.
My city hides behind me. They mutter death,
and my shadow falls as evidence of sunlight.

2 Is it possible to read this as if it were someone talking about where they came from? Or someone writing a letter? With a partner, read it to each other in different ways, trying to disguise the fact that it is a poem.

Learning checkpoint

Write three or four sentences to show the ways in which the writer uses language to communicate inner conflict. You could use these starting points if you wish:

In spite of bad things she may hear, such as …

Even the language she learned as a child …

Although she is now in a city that …

On the one hand the writer is 'free', but …

Show your skills

What evidence is there in the poem that the writer 'loves language'? Read through the poem and jot down examples of any interesting or unusual phrases. Which convey a mood or thought clearly and which remain mysterious?

Comparing poems

Taking the interesting use of language as your starting point, choose another poem from the cluster to compare with 'The Emigrée'.

GETTING IT INTO WRITING

Drawing upon all the information and ideas you now have, write two or three paragraphs (about 150–200 words) discussing how the émigrée's conflict is communicated, focusing on **one** of the three verses.

Your response

How does it affect your response to the poem to learn that the poet, Carol Rumens, was not born in a foreign city, but in London?

The worst news I receive of it cannot break
my original view, the bright, filled paperweight.

Power and conflict

14 Kamikaze

GETTING STARTED – THE POEM AND YOU

This poem expects the reader to understand the term *kamikaze*. Have you heard of it before? Read the Contexts box to find out more.

 Contexts

The word kamikaze is Japanese for 'divine wind', and is the unofficial name for the suicide attacks made by Japanese pilots in the Second World War, when Special Attack Unit pilots would fly bombs directly into ships. Flying a kamikaze mission was portrayed as a great honour by the Japanese government, and it was claimed that there were many volunteers, although some modern critics have argued that perhaps not every kamikaze soldier would have been willing. By the end of the war, nearly 4,000 kamikaze pilots had died.

KAMIKAZE

Her father embarked at sunrise
with a flask of water, a samurai sword
in the cockpit, a shaven head
full of powerful incantations
and enough fuel for a one-way   5
journey into history

but half way there, she thought,
recounting it later to her children,
he must have looked far down
at the little fishing boats   10
strung out like bunting
on a green-blue translucent sea

and beneath them, arcing in swathes
like a huge flag waved first one way
then the other in a figure of eight,   15
the dark shoals of fishes
flashing silver as their bellies
swivelled towards the sun

and remembered how he and
his brothers waiting on the shore   20
built cairns of pearl-grey pebbles
to see whose withstood longest
the turbulent inrush of breakers
bringing their father's boat safe

— yes, grandfather's boat — safe   25
to the shore, salt-sodden, awash
with cloud-marked mackerel,
black crabs, feathery prawns,
the loose silver of whitebait and once
a tuna, the dark prince, muscular, dangerous.   30

And though he came back
my mother never spoke again
in his presence, nor did she meet his eyes
and the neighbours too, they treated him
as though he no longer existed,   35
only we children still chattered and laughed

till gradually we too learned
to be silent, to live as though
he had never returned, that this
was no longer the father we loved.   40
And sometimes, she said, he must have wondered
which had been the better way to die.

Beatrice Garland

GETTING CLOSER – FOCUS ON DETAILS

First impressions

1 Read the poem. What do you think it is about? Discuss the following words with a partner and decide on the three most appropriate terms – or provide your own.

cowardice	family	disgrace	memories
home	death	honour	failure

2 How important are women and children in the poem, compared with the men?

Interpreting themes, ideas, attitudes and feelings

1 The poem covers a number of periods of time, people and generations. Can you sort them out? Create a tree diagram to show the relationships.

- The pilot
- The pilot's brothers
- Grandfather – a fisherman
- The writer
- Brothers and sisters
- The writer's mother/pilot's daughter.

2 Put the events into **chronological** order:

a The pilot embarks.
b The pilot turns round.
c Neighbours ostracise him.
d The daughter (the writer's mother) does not speak in his presence.
e The daughter thinks about what must have happened.
f The pilot flies over the sea.
g The pilot, when younger, rescues his father's boat.
h The writer writes about it.
i We (the writer and siblings) also become silent.

PUTTING DETAILS TO USE

Analysing language, form and structure

1 The poem is written in three sentences: a very long one, followed by two others in decreasing length. What effect does this have when you are:

a reading it
b speaking it?

The long middle part of the poem comprises a description of the sea seen from above, together with memories of the fishing catch. Look at the lines from 'fishing boats' down to 'dangerous'. Pick out five or six words and phrases that you think create an effective picture or pictures for the reader.

3 Compare your selections with a partner and then make a composite list. Try to give a reason why that description works well. For example:

Example	Comment	Is there a term for this?
'little fishing boats / strung out like bunting'	From above they look like the little triangular flags on a string of bunting	simile
'turbulent inrush'	The words not only describe the way the waves come in but also make a similar sound.	onomatopoeia

Show your skills

Assess your progress

Make a checklist of what you have learned so far. Make two columns, one for things you definitely know and one for things you are fairly sure of. The second column may be things you have inferred or 'read between the lines' and may be phrased as questions. For example:

What I know	What I wonder
This is a poem about a kamikaze pilot who turns back.	The writer emphasises the word 'safe' – is that the reason he turned back?
It does not have a formal structure.	
It describes …	The sea is very important in the poem. Is this because …

the turbulent inrush of breakers
bringing their father's boat safe

Write three or four sentences based on some of your notes from the table, exploring the role of motivation (why people do things) in the poem.

Reading skills to show in your writing	Examples of starting points
Understanding: understanding is a grasp of the basics of what the poem is about, which could be people, events, situations or places.	*The father becomes a kamikaze pilot because it is expected of him. In his situation . . .*
Interpreting themes, ideas, attitudes and feelings: when you interpret, you move from your understanding of the poem, to show what your understanding means to you or to someone else.	*The expectations of the pilot's family are . . .* *As a result, when he returns . . .*
Implied meanings: this is where you understand more than is obviously stated and you 'read between the lines'.	*For the rest of his life, it is implied . . .*

GETTING IT INTO WRITING

Write a paragraph about the last two verses, explaining what has happened and exploring what you think the poet is communicating to you. You may like to read these two samples beforehand and see how far you think they fulfil the task.

The kamikaze pilot returns home to discover that instead of being welcomed he is almost outlawed because he has not fulfilled their expectations of honour and duty. Eventually even the children learn to be silent when he is around. He is as cut off from life as he would have been had he never come back.

After the pilot returns home, no one will speak to him except the children who continue chattering and laughing until they are taught to be silent. Even the neighbours ignore him. It is as though they are pretending he is dead. The poem implies that he would have been better off dead.

Comparing poems

This is an exercise in empathy – trying to get inside someone else's experience. A number of poems in this collection do the same thing, for example 'Bayonet Charge', 'Poppies' and 'War Photographer'. For each of these poems, consider how successful the poet is in attempting to 'be' someone else or to speak with their voice.

GETTING CREATIVE

Putting yourself into an unfamiliar situation

In the poem, the writer is not only writing about a kamikaze pilot, she is imagining it from the point of view of the pilot's daughter. Choose one of the following and write a paragraph from the point of view of someone who knew them. You will probably need to carry out some research beforehand.

- a   The wife of an Antarctic explorer
- b   The boyfriend of Amy Johnson
- c   The mother or father of an astronaut
- d   Shakespeare's son or daughter.

Your response

Do you think the treatment of the father is cruel? Or is it impossible to judge a situation that is so different from our own experience?

Power and conflict
15 Checking Out Me History

GETTING STARTED – THE POEM AND YOU

Think about the history you have been taught in school. Which historical events do you remember most clearly? Make a list of the topics you can recall. Why do you remember those particular topics?

GETTING CLOSER – FOCUS ON DETAILS

First impressions

1 Read or listen to 'Checking Out Me History'. The poem is written in a **dialect** called Creole, which may be unfamiliar at first but soon becomes easy to follow. Apart from using a 'd' sound in place of 'th', what other variations do you notice?

2 In pairs or threes, try reading the poem as if it was written in **standard English**. For example change 'Dem' to 'They', 'bout' to 'about' and so on, and insert any words that you feel are 'missing' from a standard English version. Is it possible to make the poem work speaking it like this? What tone of voice is appropriate?

Interpreting themes, ideas, attitudes and feelings

'Dem' becomes one of the most important words in the poem, but 'dem' are never given a name.

Think about the well-used phrase 'Them and Us'. Many people will use 'they' to refer to a group that has power: the government, bosses, perhaps even the people running your school. 'They've put up the price of …', 'They don't care about us …', and so on.

Discuss these questions with a partner and agree a brief answer to each:

a   Who are 'dem'?
b   What do they want to tell?
c   How does the writer feel about that?
d   What do they not tell him?
e   How does he feel about the things that he wasn't told?

ℹ Contexts

John Agard grew up in the West Indies, and moved to Britain in 1977, to follow his dream of becoming a writer. In 2013 he was awarded the Queen's Gold Medal for Poetry.

The theme of cultural identity is one that he explores widely in his work. Coming from Guyana, with its history of slavery and colonisation, gives his feelings about 'them' and 'us' even more power. His favourite place to write is in the pub with a pint of Guinness!

CHECKING OUT ME HISTORY

Dem tell me
Dem tell me
Wha dem want to tell me

Bandage up me eye with me own history
Blind me to me own identity   5

Dem tell me bout 1066 and all dat
dem tell me bout Dick Whittington and he cat
But Toussaint L'Ouverture
no dem never tell me bout dat

Toussaint   10
a slave
with vision
lick back
Napoleon
battalion   15
and first Black
Republic born
Toussaint de thorn
to de French
Toussaint de beacon   20
of de Haitian Revolution

Dem tell me bout de man who discover de balloon
and de cow who jump over de moon
Dem tell me bout de dish run away with de spoon
but dem never tell me bout Nanny de maroon   25

Nanny
See-far woman
of mountain dream
fire-woman struggle
hopeful stream   30
to freedom river

Dem tell me bout Lord Nelson and Waterloo
but dem never tell me bout Shaka de great Zulu
Dem tell me bout Columbus and 1492
but what happen to de Caribs and de Arawaks too 35

Dem tell me bout Florence Nightingale and she lamp
and how Robin Hood used to camp
Dem tell me bout ole King Cole was a merry ole soul
but dem never tell me bout Mary Seacole

From Jamaica 40
she travel far
to the Crimean War
she volunteer to go
and even when de British said no
she still brave the Russian snow 45
a healing star
among the wounded
a yellow sunrise
to the dying

Dem tell me 50
Dem tell me wha dem want to tell me
But now I checking out me own history
I carving out me identity

John Agard

Listen to the poem on Cambridge Elevate

159

PUTTING DETAILS TO USE

Analysing language, form and structure

The poem is shown in two styles: normal and italic. They could be said to be two different voices: they certainly have different tones. How do the parts written in italic font differ from those in normal font? Match the different parts of the poem to what you notice about their language and tone. Add two examples of your own to the second column:

Those in normal font style …	… are about other people.
	… are about the writer.
	… have a jerky rhythm.
	… have a smoother rhythm.
	… have an angry tone.
Those in italic font style …	… use lots of repetition.
	… use positive words and phrases.
	… use rhymes.
	…
	…

Show your skills

Look at these examples of students' writing and see if you can pick out:

a   where the student has moved from the explicit to notice something implicit
b   where the student has moved from explaining (saying what the poem is about/ the poem's meaning) to exploring (finding interesting things about the way the meaning is expressed).

A   'Checking Out Me History' is about Agard's reflections on being taught history, which ignored anything to do with him and where he comes from. He was taught about famous people like Nelson but not about people from the West Indies such as Mary Seacole who worked, like Florence Nightingale, as a nurse in the Crimean War. His history has been ignored. To make his point even more strongly, he writes in the Creole form of English from his native Guyana and constantly refers to those who taught him history as 'dem'.

B   He makes fun of being taught about nursery-rhyme characters that mean nothing to him but there is a serious purpose underneath lines such as 'Dem tell me bout Columbus and 1492 / but what happen to de Caribs and de Arawaks too' as the original inhabitants of the West Indies were practically wiped out by the colonising Europeans who brought in African slaves to work on their land instead.

C   When he writes about historical figures from African or West Indian culture, his language becomes more positive and he begins to use interesting imagery such as 'a healing star / among the wounded / a yellow sunrise / to the dying'.

Learning checkpoint

Write a few bullet points to sum up what you know about Agard's poem so far. You can use these starting phrases if you wish:

- Agard's poem is about …
- He feels that …
- The language of the poem is …
- There are two different 'voices'. The first voice …
- The second voice …
- The effect of the poem is …

GETTING IT INTO WRITING

Look closely at lines 6–21 (or 22–31 or 36–49). Using them as your starting point, write between 100 and 200 words to explain to someone who has not read the poem how Agard uses two voices to make his point about history. You might begin: 'Agard writes his poem in two different voices, standard English and Creole. He uses standard English to …'

Comparing poems

The characters in 'Checking Out Me History' and 'The Emigrée' feel separate in some way. How do they express their feelings of being out of place in their poems?

Read the following extracts from students' writing and discuss them with a partner. Where would you want to see evidence from the poems? Where have the writers gone beyond what is obvious to talk about what is implied? Finally, is there any sense of a student speculating what might be the case?

A   In 'Checking Out Me History', John Agard expresses his dissatisfaction with the way history has been taught. He compares historical figures who are relevant to him and his culture with the ones he has been taught about in school. Carol Rumens describes the feelings of being in an environment which is unfamiliar, even though the city she recalls is so far back in time.

B   The way they express their feelings is very different. Agard makes his feeling of separateness clear from the start through his use of non-standard English. He alternates styles within the poem and even shows it by changing fonts. Rumens shows two conflicting sides by putting positive and negative images next to each other throughout the poem. Both writers refer to unknown people in authority in a negative way – Agard talks about those who taught history as 'dem'/'them'. Rumens talks about 'they' who in some way seem to threaten her.

C   Agard's tone is one of controlled anger whereas Rumens' tone is more regretful and quiet. Agard seems to know very clearly what he thinks, but Rumens' poem conveys confusion as if she misses her home town and cannot go back to it, but neither does she feel comfortable where she is.

GETTING CREATIVE

Balloon debate

A balloon debate involves a number of characters in the basket of a balloon that is losing height. One or two characters have to go over the side. Each character has two minutes to explain why they should stay in – their importance to history, their good character, and so on.

1 Each of you should spend some time researching the historical figures mentioned by Agard:

- Toussaint L'Ouverture
- Nanny of the Maroons
- Lord Nelson
- Shaka Zulu
- Christopher Columbus
- Florence Nightingale
- Mary Seacole.

2 Then choose volunteers to represent each historical figure and to give a short speech. After all the speeches, the class votes via a secret ballot. Give each figure a score from 7 (the highest) to 1 (the lowest). After you add up all the points, the two figures with the lowest total score must leave the balloon!

Your response

How do you feel about the history you have been taught? Does it include anything about the place or area you come from – or that your parents or grandparents came from? How would you go about finding more information?

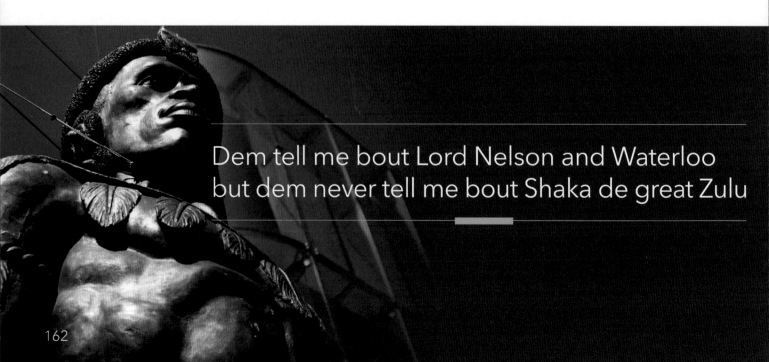

Dem tell me bout Lord Nelson and Waterloo
but dem never tell me bout Shaka de great Zulu

Power and conflict
16 Comparing poems

What you have to do

If you are studying Cluster 2 'Power and conflict' from the anthology, then in Section B of your poetry exam you will need to compare two poems from this cluster.

- One poem from Cluster 2 will be printed for you on the exam paper.
- Once you know the question, you will need to choose another poem from Cluster 2 to compare the named poem with.
- You will not have your anthology with you in the exam room.
- You will have around 45 minutes to write your comparison.

The comparison question

The question you are asked in the exam will give you a focus for your comparison. For example:

> Compare <u>the ways poets present</u> <u>ideas</u> <u>about power</u> in '<u>Ozymandias</u>' and **one** other poem from 'Power and conflict'.
>
> **[30 marks]**

Read the question carefully and focus your comparison on what the question asks. The focus in this question is on the underlined words and phrases.

The focus of the question might vary depending on the poem. For example you might be asked about the **ideas** or **attitudes** in the poem, and the focus might be on ideas about power, conflict in war, or another aspect of the poem. The themes of power and conflict may both be present within an individual poem. When thinking about conflict, be aware that conflict can be external (physical) or internal (mental/ psychological).

Until you see the poem and the question, you will not know the focus of your comparison. However, your study of the poems in your GCSE course should mean that you know each poem in the cluster so well that you will feel prepared and confident. Show your skills by choosing a poem to compare that gives you lots to say in response to the focus of the question.

Comparing poems

Comparing poems simply means writing about **similarities** and **differences** in the **content** and **style** of two poems.

The most obvious similarity is that the two poems from Cluster 2 will be about power and/or conflict. The similarities and differences that matter are **what** the poets have to say about power and/or conflict (content), and **how** they say it (style).

The **content** is what's in the poem. Depending on the poem, this might include:

- situations, experiences, people, places
- ideas, thoughts, feelings, attitudes, perspectives, contexts
- **setting**, **atmosphere**.

The **style** is how the poem is written. You will write about the poem's style in relation to its content, and analyse the choices the poet has made to express their ideas. This might include:

- use of language – tone and techniques
- structure
- form, and the pattern of rhythm and rhyme.

Similarities and differences

Comparing two poems can help you to understand each poem more clearly, as you often notice different things when you explore poems side by side. It's similar in some ways to when you buy a new mobile phone or some new trainers and look at a variety of features side by side to make the best choice.

When you are thinking about comparison, let the poems speak for themselves. Students sometimes tie themselves in knots inventing similarities that cannot easily be supported by evidence from the texts.

It can be more productive to think about differences than similarities, though you are encouraged to do both. If you think about style as being something individual (in the same way that styles of dress and styles of architecture can be individual, for instance), it is likely that you will find more differences than similarities in style in poetry, too.

How you will be assessed

The Assessment Objectives (AOs) outline the skills you need to demonstrate in order to be successful. In the anthology question the three AOs are:

AO1: Read, understand and respond to texts. Students should be able to:

- maintain a critical style and develop an informed personal response
- use textual references, including quotations, to support and illustrate interpretations.

AO2: Analyse the language, form and structure used by a writer to create meanings and effects, using relevant subject terminology where appropriate.

AO3: Show understanding of the relationships between texts and the contexts in which they were written.

How these resources support you

In this book, you will develop your skills in each of the Assessment Objectives above as you:

- explore each poem in Cluster 2 and develop a focused response that will help you when it comes to comparing poems
- consider possible links between the poems and develop ways of comparing and writing about them.

Developing skills in comparing poems

POEM PAIR 1: 'BAYONET CHARGE' AND 'EXPOSURE'

In this section you will develop your skills in linking and comparing poems by using the following question:

Compare the ways poets present attitudes to conflict in 'Bayonet Charge' and **one** other poem from 'Power and conflict'.

This reminds you that you must explain the ways the poets use techniques to present attitudes.

This tells you what aspects of content you must write about.

The 'named' poem will always be printed on the question paper.

Choosing a poem to compare

1 Which poems might be suitable to compare with 'Bayonet Charge' to show the ways different poets present attitudes towards conflict?

Remember that poems on a similar theme that have contrasting features offer good writing opportunities, just as ones with similar features do.

2 Discuss possible choices with a partner. There are several war poems that might provide good links.

3 To develop your skills in preparing and writing an answer, let's say the poem you have chosen to compare with 'Bayonet Charge' is Wilfred Owen's 'Exposure'.

Reread the two poems in Cluster 2 Units 6 and 8. If you have studied these poems already and completed the focused responses, they will be very useful for your comparison, so refresh your memory.

Comparing content

1 On a sheet of paper, create two columns headed 'Bayonet Charge' by Ted Hughes and 'Exposure' by Wilfred Owen. With a partner, discuss the following aspects of each poem:

- who is speaking
- in what situation
- what happens – how the situation develops
- how the setting and the soldiers' situation are described (might 'Exposure' be an appropriate title for either poem?)
- the **viewpoint** from which the poem is presented
- the thoughts, feelings and attitudes of the people in the poem
- why you think the poet chose to write the poem.

King, honour, human dignity, etcetera
Dropped like luxuries in a yelling alarm

(From 'Bayonet Charge')

2 Now make notes on similarities and differences between these aspects in the two columns. Both poems are set on First World War battlefields. In comparing thoughts, feelings and attitudes, it might help you to explore and compare verse 3 in 'Bayonet Charge' with verse 7 in 'Exposure'.

Comparing language

1 Make a list of the sense impressions (sights, sounds and so on) that the poet uses in the opening verse of 'Bayonet Charge' to make the situation 'come alive' for the reader, and discuss how they make the reader feel about the soldier's situation.

2 Ted Hughes uses a lot of verbs in his writing to communicate action. Why do you think that in the first verse of 'Bayonet Charge' the poet says 'was running' rather than 'ran', '(was) stumbling' not 'stumbled' and so on?

3 Hughes also uses a lot of similes. What do you think he is trying to get the reader to imagine by saying:

- 'He lugged a rifle numb as a smashed arm'
- 'The patriotic tear … / Sweating like molten iron from the centre of his chest'
- 'He was running / Like a man who has jumped up in the dark'
- 'his foot hung like / Statuary in mid-stride'
- 'Threw up a yellow hare that rolled like a flame'
- 'King … / Dropped like luxuries in a yelling alarm'?

4 In 'Bayonet Charge', explain how the language used in lines 10–11 and the last four lines of the poem is effective in bringing out the soldier's feelings about his situation.

5 Explain why the poet chooses to describe the hare in the last verse, and how the poet makes the description of its death powerful.

6 In looking at the content of the two poems, you will have recognised that although both are about soldiers in a war zone and both communicate the horrors of war, the poets are focusing on different situations, and the poets' different intentions lead to different styles of writing. In general terms, how would you say that Owen uses language differently from Hughes?

7 Like Hughes, Owen uses lots of **diction** and imagery in 'Exposure', which appeal strongly to the reader's senses. Find examples and explain how they make you feel about the soldiers' situation.

8 Study verse four of 'Exposure', which is rich in alliteration. How does the language used in the first line (describing the gunfire) compare with that used in the remainder of the verse (describing the snow)?

In order to appreciate the effects of the poet's use of language, you might find it helpful to read the verse aloud.

Worried by silence, sentries whisper, curious, nervous, But nothing happens.

(From 'Exposure')

9 'Exposure' is a long poem very rich in poetic language. Here is an example of how you might annotate verse one:

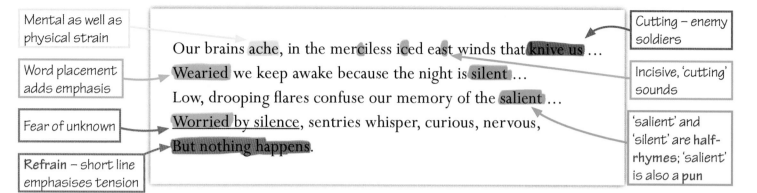

Mental as well as physical strain

Word placement adds emphasis

Fear of unknown

Refrain – short line emphasises tension

Our brains ache, in the merciless iced east winds that knive us …
Wearied we keep awake because the night is silent …
Low, drooping flares confuse our memory of the salient …
Worried by silence, sentries whisper, curious, nervous,
But nothing happens.

Cutting – enemy soldiers

Incisive, 'cutting' sounds

'salient' and 'silent' are half-rhymes; 'salient' is also a pun

Work in a pair. One student should write out and annotate key details in verse two and the other verse three. Then compare your notes.

Comparing structure and form

1 'Bayonet Charge' is written in three verses. At the end of line 9, the poet creates a slight pause as the soldier suddenly begins to think about his situation - 'he almost stopped', but the poem is almost continuous, as there are few full stops, and verses are not separated by punctuation. Hughes also uses a lot of dashes. What effects do these features have on the **pace** of the poem?

2 How effective are the opening and closing lines of 'Bayonet Charge', and why?

3 Find two good examples of Hughes' use of **enjambement** (the technique of 'overlapping' a sentence onto a new line to emphasise words and phrases at the openings of lines) and explain why they are important/effective.

4 'Exposure' is written in eight verses, with short final lines that act as a refrain. Several lines are deliberately unfinished, punctuated with an ellipsis at the end. How do these features affect the pace or 'flow' of the poem?

5 The last line is usually used as a refrain to emphasise the lack of action. It is not used in the same way in each verse. What are the effects of Owen's variation of the pattern?

6 Often a poet will describe a situation and then introduce a key thought or 'message' at the end of the poem. In 'Exposure', this seems to happen in the penultimate verse, where the poet explains why the soldiers feel they are in the trenches fighting the Germans. The poem could easily have ended here. Why, then, do you think that Owen goes back to describing the scene in the trenches in the very last verse? What is the significance of the opening word 'Tonight'?

Writing a comparison

Using your work on this poem, develop your skills in writing a comparison by responding to the following question, using 'Exposure' as the poem to compare:

> Compare the ways poets present attitudes to conflict in 'Bayonet Charge' and **one** other poem from 'Power and conflict'.

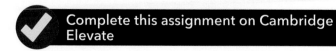

Complete this assignment on Cambridge Elevate

POEM PAIR 2: 'STORM ON THE ISLAND' AND 'OZYMANDIAS'

In this section you will develop your skills in linking and comparing poems by using the following question:

> Compare how poets present attitudes to power and conflict in 'Storm on the Island' and **one** other poem from 'Power and conflict'.

This reminds you that you must explain how the poets use techniques to present attitudes.

This tells you what aspects of content you must write about.

The 'named' poem will always be printed on the question paper.

Choosing a poem to compare

1 Which poems might be suitable to compare with 'Storm on the Island' to show how different poets present attitudes towards power and conflict?

Remember that poems on a similar theme that have contrasting features offer good writing opportunities, just as ones with similar features do.

2 Discuss possible choices with a partner. A number of poems in the anthology explore very different kinds of conflict.

3 To develop your skills in preparing and writing an answer, let's say the poem you have chosen to compare with 'Storm on the Island' is Percy Bysshe Shelley's 'Ozymandias'.

Reread the two poems in Cluster 2 Units 1 and 7. If you have studied these poems already and completed the focused responses, they will be very useful for your comparison, so refresh your memory.

We just sit tight while wind dives
And strafes invisibly. Space is a salvo

(From 'Storm on the Island')

Comparing content

1 On a sheet of paper, create two columns headed 'Storm on the Island' by Seamus Heaney and 'Ozymandias' by Percy Bysshe Shelley. With a partner, discuss the following aspects of each poem:

- who is speaking
- to whom, if anyone
- the setting
- what happens – how the situation and ideas are developed
- the viewpoint from which the poem is presented
- the thoughts, feelings and attitudes of the people in the poem
- why you think the poet chose to write the poem.

2 Now make notes on similarities and differences between these aspects in the two columns.

3 Describe the places where you imagine the two poems are set. You might like to draw rough sketches of each scene, labelling them with descriptive words from the poems.

4 What types of power would you say are being explored in the poems?

5 Which of the following words might be used to describe the speakers in the two poems? You might think that some apply to neither. Remember to justify your interpretations with supporting detail from the text.

overawed
practical
frightened
unflappable
intimidated
philosophical
boastful
unemotional
humble

6 The speaker's tone of voice in 'Storm on the Island' is quite conversational, and they seem to be addressing someone in particular. What do phrases like 'as you see', 'you know what I mean', and 'You might think' suggest about the situation and experiences of the person who is being addressed?

7 Who do you think the speaker in 'Ozymandias' might be addressing?

Comparing language

1 Study Heaney's word choices in the first five lines of 'Storm on the Island': 'squat', 'sink', 'rock', 'stacks', 'stooks'. The poet uses alliteration to emphasise a number of these words. Can you say anything else about the sounds of these words? Do they help to give an impression of the character of the speaker?

2 Explain the meaning and comment on the effectiveness of:

a 'This wizened earth has never troubled us / With hay'

b 'leaves and branches / Can raise a tragic chorus in a gale / So that you listen to the thing you fear / Forgetting that it pummels your house too'

c 'spits like a tame cat / Turned savage'.

3 Make a list of the words (in the second half of the poem) that are connected with war. What is the effect on the reader of Heaney's choice of military imagery to describe the weather?

4 Make a list of all the adjectives used in 'Ozymandias'. Do they have anything in common? What sort of atmosphere do they create?

5 In 'Ozymandias', the speaker suggests that the sculptor captured the character and attitudes of Ozymandias very faithfully ('its sculptor well those passions read'). How do the descriptive details in lines 4–6, and the inscription on the pedestal create a vivid impression of the king's character?

6 In Shelley's poem, the speaker uses a calm and measured tone. What do you think this suggests about his attitude towards Ozymandias and his life?

7 Make a list of the words and phrases that emphasise the idea of destruction in 'Ozymandias', and say whether you think they are effective.

8 The poet deliberately inverts (turns around) the natural word order in the last three lines of 'Ozymandias'. What effect do you think he intended this to have on the reader? If the sentence had read 'The lone and level sands stretch far away / Round the decay / Of that colossal wreck, boundless and bare', would the ending have been as effective?

Comparing structure and form

1 In 'Storm on the Island', do you think that the opening phrase is an effective way of starting the poem? Why?

2 Poems usually build up towards a climax that presents a key idea in the poem. Heaney uses 'huge nothing' in the last line of his poem, which is an apparent contradiction.

   a Can you explain what it means?
   b Is it an effective way to end the poem?

3 In 'Storm on the Island', 'But' in line 11 seems to signal a change in the direction of the poem. How does the description in lines 1–10 have a different focus from what Heaney emphasises about life on the island in the rest of the poem?

4 Heaney places the word 'Blast' at the opening of line 7 to give it a powerful emphasis. Find and comment on the effectiveness of other examples of enjambement in his poem.

5 Like Heaney, Shelley uses enjambement to good effect, for example in lines 3, 4, 7, 12 and 13. Why are the words and phrases Shelley chooses to emphasise in this way important to the poem's meaning?

6 In 'Ozymandias', what do you notice about the opening and closing words of line 3 and the structure (how the words are organised) of line 8?

7 An important structural feature of a sonnet is a **volta** or 'turning-point' – a point in the poem at which we can see the poet 'changing direction' in developing ideas. In 'Ozymandias' it seems to be after line 8, signalled by 'And' – how does the emphasis/focus of the poem change after this point?

8 How successful do you think the last sentence of 'Ozymandias' is as a climax to the poem?

Writing a comparison

Using your work on this poem, develop your skills in writing a comparison by responding to the following question, using 'Ozymandias' as the poem to compare:

> Compare how poets present attitudes to power and conflict in 'Storm on the Island' and **one** other poem from 'Power and conflict.'

 Complete this assignment on Cambridge Elevate

POEM PAIR 3: 'KAMIKAZE' AND 'THE CHARGE OF THE LIGHT BRIGADE'

In this section you will develop your skills in linking and comparing poems by using the following question:

Compare <u>how</u> poets present <u>attitudes to power and conflict</u> in 'Kamikaze' and **one** other poem from 'Power and conflict'.

> This reminds you that you must explain how the poets use techniques to present attitudes.

> This tells you what aspects of content you must write about.

> The 'named' poem will always be printed on the question paper.

Choosing a poem to compare

1 Which poems might be suitable to compare with 'Kamikaze' to show how different poets present attitudes towards power and conflict?

Remember that poems on a similar theme that have contrasting features offer good writing opportunities, just as ones with similar features do.

2 Discuss possible choices with a partner. There are several war poems in the anthology that might provide good links.

3 To develop your skills in preparing and writing an answer, let's say the poem you have chosen to compare with 'Kamikaze' is Tennyson's 'The Charge of the Light Brigade'.

Reread the two poems in Cluster 2 Units 5 and 14. If you have studied these poems already and completed the focused responses, they will be very useful for your comparison, so refresh your memory.

Comparing content

1 On a sheet of paper, create two columns headed 'Kamikaze' by Beatrice Garland and 'The Charge of the Light Brigade' by Alfred Lord Tennyson. With a partner, discuss the following aspects of each poem:

- who is speaking
- in what situation and setting
- the historical and cultural context
- what happens – how the poem develops
- the viewpoint from which the poem is presented
- the thoughts and feelings of the people in the poem
- why you think the poet chose to write the poem.

2 Now make notes on similarities and differences between these aspects in the two columns.

the turbulent inrush of breakers
bringing their father's boat safe

(From 'Kamikaze')

3 In verse one of 'Kamikaze', how do the descriptions of the pilot and his 'possessions' provide important information for the reader? 'Embarked' is quite a formal word. What does this suggest?

4 The children's mother says 'he must have …' in verse two. What does this suggest?

5 Why is the description of the scene the pilot saw as he looked down from his journey while crossing the sea (verses two and three) important in helping the reader to understand his behaviour?

6 Describe and explain the attitudes of the pilot's wife, the neighbours and the children to their father (described in the last two verses). How did the children's attitudes change, and why? Which of the following statements do you agree with and why?

Their attitudes changed because:

a they had learned more about the nature of 'honour'

b they saw their mother as a role model

c they were affected by pressure from their neighbours

d as a result of other people's treatment of their father, they didn't have opportunities to maintain a close relationship.

7 In verse four, Garland describes how the pilot and his brothers helped to bring his own father back safely from a different kind of 'mission' – a fishing trip on a rough sea. Why do you think that the poet mentions this?

8 In 'The Charge of the Light Brigade', explain what the soldiers think and feel about the situation they find themselves in.

9 How do you think that society's attitude towards bravery and honour in Tennyson's poem is similar to or different from that explored in 'Kamikaze'?

10 In the last verse of 'The Charge of the Light Brigade', Tennyson says:

O the wild charge they made!

All the world wonder'd.

Honour the charge they made!

Honour the Light Brigade,

Which of the following statements do you think best sums up the speaker's attitude towards the cavalry charge? He thinks that:

a the men should be admired for the courage they showed

b the charge was foolish rather than brave

c the cavalrymen should have ignored the rash orders they had been given

d the men were heroic, but the officers' strategy was foolish.

Comparing language

1 Beatrice Garland uses a lot of descriptive detail to create a vivid picture of the natural scene in verses two to five. You might annotate part of verse two as follows:

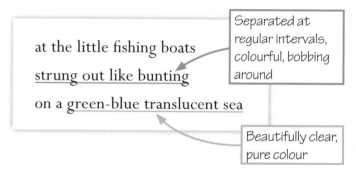

Work in a pair. One student should write out and annotate key details in verse three and the other verse five. Each should annotate key descriptive details; then compare your notes.

2 How does 'turbulent inrush of breakers' convey the sight and sound of the sea?

3 In 'The Charge of the Light Brigade', Tennyson is describing action rather than a scene, and there is not a lot of descriptive detail. The few images he uses describe the situation in general and are more abstract; they could even be said to be **clichés**:

- 'the valley of Death' (is there a biblical echo?)
- 'jaws of Death'
- 'mouth of Hell'.

What are the effects of these images on the reader?

4 The fourth verse describes the climax of the charge. Make a list of all the verbs used to emphasis the violent action at this point.

Comparing structure and form

1 The structure of 'Kamikaze' is made clear by the change to italic lettering in the last two verses, which indicates a 'shift' in the poem. Complete the following sentences:

a   In the last two verses the poet focuses on …
b   Her intention is to make the reader think/feel …

2 How does the last verse move ideas further on from the previous one?

3 The poem moves towards a concise and forceful climax. Do you think the last two lines are an effective, thought-provoking way of ending the poem?

4 The numbered verses in 'The Charge of the Light Brigade' indicate the narrative nature of the poem – the poem has a clear chronological sequence. There is a lot of obvious repetition, a regular rhyme scheme and frequent alliteration. What effect do these features have on the pace of the poem? (Reading the poem aloud might help you to appreciate the effect that Tennyson is trying to achieve.)

5 The poem uses a refrain, but 'six hundred' is used differently by the poet in different verses. Trace the uses of the refrain through the poem and consider how the changes affect the mood of the poem at various points in the action.

6 How effectively does Tennyson use punctuation in the last verse, the climax of the poem, to influence the reader's attitude towards events and convey a 'message'?

Writing a comparison

Using your work on this poem, develop your skills in writing a comparison by responding to the following question, using 'The Charge of the Light Brigade' as the poem to compare:

> Compare how poets present attitudes to power and conflict in 'Kamikaze' and **one** other poem from 'Power and conflict'.

Complete this assignment on Cambridge Elevate

Into the valley of Death
Rode the six hundred.

(From 'The Charge of the Light Brigade')

EXAMPLE RESPONSE: 'LONDON' AND THE EXTRACT FROM 'THE PRELUDE'

In this section you will develop your skills in linking and comparing poems by writing a response to the following question. You will then study a good example response.

> Compare how poets present attitudes towards power and conflict in 'London' and **one** other poem from 'Power and conflict'.

The poem chosen for comparison is the extract from William Wordsworth's 'The Prelude'.

Making notes

The following example uses the model of annotating the 'named' poem, along with brief notes on the poem chosen from the rest of the anthology cluster. You might have a preferred way of making notes that works for you. With these notes, notice that:

- no complete sentences are used
- notes can be made very concisely when based on annotation
- no quotations are noted on the 'remembered' poem (this might take too much time and they could be added when writing).

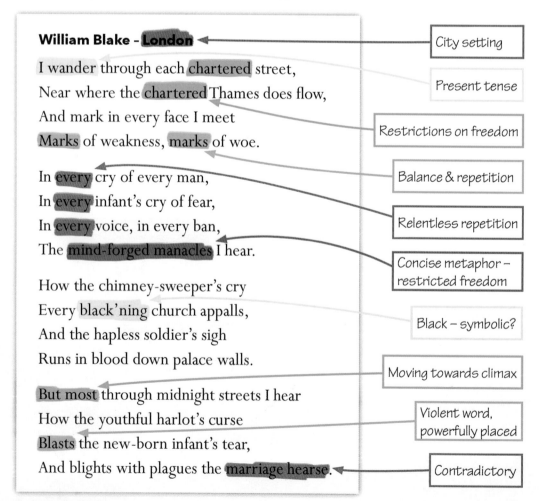

William Blake – London — City setting

I wander through each chartered street, — Present tense

Near where the chartered Thames does flow,

And mark in every face I meet — Restrictions on freedom

Marks of weakness, marks of woe. — Balance & repetition

In every cry of every man,

In every infant's cry of fear, — Relentless repetition

In every voice, in every ban,

The mind-forged manacles I hear. — Concise metaphor – restricted freedom

How the chimney-sweeper's cry

Every black'ning church appalls, — Black – symbolic?

And the hapless soldier's sigh

Runs in blood down palace walls. — Moving towards climax

But most through midnight streets I hear

How the youthful harlot's curse — Violent word, powerfully placed

Blasts the new-born infant's tear,

And blights with plagues the marriage hearse. — Contradictory

Overall: monotonous rhythm and dismal-sounding vocabulary

174

William Wordsworth – The Prelude extract

- Rural setting

- Natural world attractive but later threatening (shift in tone) – contrasting vocabulary

- Guilt

- Insignificance of humans

- Visual appeal

- Vocabulary emphasises power of nature

- No rhyme, and long, majestic sentences

- First-person narrative – describes personal experience.

Getting it into writing

1 Reread the extract from 'The Prelude' (Cluster 2 Unit 3). If you have studied these poems already and completed the focused responses, they will be very useful for your comparison, so refresh your memory.

It may help you to know that both these poets were 'Romantic' poets, writing around the end of the 18th century. Romantic poets tended to value the rural (country) environment above the urban (city) one. Wordsworth attempted to use 'colloquial' rather than formal poetic language, and once described good poetry as 'the spontaneous overflow of powerful feelings'.

2 Now write your response to the following question, using the extract from 'The Prelude' as the paired poem:

Compare how poets present attitudes to power and conflict in 'London' and **one** other poem from 'Power and conflict'.

Use the notes above to help you, but add your own ideas.

You could write in timed conditions for 35 minutes (assuming you would spend about 10 minutes making notes).

Paired assessment

1 When you have completed your response, exchange it with a partner. Then answer these questions, giving examples in each case:

a Has your partner made similar points to you?

b Has either of you made points that the other hasn't?

c Have all points been made clearly? If not, check what your partner intended to say.

d Are there things you disagree about?

e Have all points been supported by references to the poems? If not, suggest which details might have been used to back up the points you make.

f Have all references to the poets' techniques shown the use and effect of the technique?

Now read the example response.

One summer evening (led by her) I found
A little boat tied to a willow tree

Example response

In 'London', Blake describes how when walking around the city he experiences a dismal, depressing environment inhabited by unhappy people: 'And mark in every face I meet / Marks of weakness, marks of woe.' ✔ On his travels he witnesses a range of social problems, such as prostitution and child poverty, with young boys used as chimney-sweeps. Young women, presumably drawn into prostitution by poverty, curse rather than rejoice at the birth of their children, and a child enters the world with few prospects of happiness, only a 'cry of fear'. The poet repeatedly uses the word 'chartered' to criticise laws that protect the privileges of some people while condemning others to poverty. A river is a natural force that flows uncontrolled, but Blake, exaggerating, sees even the Thames as 'chartered'. Blake sums up his attitude and feelings in line 8 using the powerful metaphor of 'mind-forged manacles'. People's minds should be free, but their intelligence has been used to create 'manacles', restrictions that are heavy and too oppressive to shake off.

The poet uses words that give a negative impression of the city: 'weakness', 'woe', 'black'ning', 'blights', 'plagues' and so on. He makes a strong appeal to the reader's emotions with phrases like 'new-born infant's tear', 'hapless soldier's sigh', 'youthful harlot's curse'. He focuses on the young because he feels their future is blighted. Repetition is one of the poem's most effective techniques, especially the relentless repetition of 'every', which suggests lack of hope and contributes to the monotonous rhythm of the poem. The neatly balanced 'Marks of weakness, marks of woe' is especially effective, as alliteration further emphasises the phrases. The climax (prepared for by 'But most' at the beginning of the final verse) is very powerful. The **oxymoron** 'the marriage-hearse' implies that marriage should be a source of optimism, but in this society it is blighted, plagued from the start, and its joys short-lived. The regular rhyme scheme adds to the monotonous rhythm of the poem. ✔

The most obvious contrast between 'London' and 'The Prelude' is in their settings, since Wordsworth describes what begins as an innocent adventure in a country environment

> ✔ Points are supported by quotations/references to the text

> ✔ Points are organised into content/style sections

but develops into a frightening experience that has a profound effect on his view of nature. Blake's poem does not really develop or suggest change, so much as present an impression of urban life and reinforce it. The change in Wordsworth's poem comes after the first 20 lines, which create a harmonious picture of the relationship between the speaker and nature: the circles created by the boat 'glitter idly'; the rock is an 'elfin pinnace' (hardly threatening!), and the boat glides 'like a swan'. The fact that the boat was in its 'usual home' sounds comforting, and the speaker feels in control as he rows to reach a 'chosen point' with an 'unswerving line'. Then the mood changes and the rock becomes 'a huge peak, black and huge', a 'grim shape' that 'towered' over him, like a creature stalking him. For some time after the incident the speaker cannot look at nature in the same way, after becoming aware of the mysteries and power of the universe, which are 'a trouble' to his dreams. Maybe he feels a sense of guilt, as at the outset of the poem he describes taking the boat as 'an act of stealth / And troubled pleasure'. Blake criticises the city; Wordsworth creates a positive view of the country, despite the unnerving nature of his experience.

> Notice that the writer found more differences than similarities

As already mentioned, the descriptive language used in the first and second stages of the poem creates a contrast that reflects the change in the speaker's mood. He also uses personification effectively to convey the threat the mountain seems to pose: 'head', 'like a living thing / Strode after me'. He feels he is being followed by a monster. Wordsworth uses a free-verse form, which creates a conversational effect – like a person telling an anecdote, and sometimes uses the flexibility of the verse form to emphasise important words and phrases at the openings of lines (for example 'upreared' and 'towered' to suggest how threatening the peak appears). You can see a clear development in the structure of the poem, as it begins with pleasant description, moves on to describe the fearful incident, and concludes with some reflection on the nature of the experience and how deeply the speaker was affected.

> Notice the paragraph structure is:
> - Poem 1 content
> - Poem 1 style
> - Poem 2 content
> - Poem 2 style.
>
> Another good option would be:
> - Poem 1 content
> - Poem 2 content
> - Poem 1 style
> - Poem 2 style.

2 An example response is not a 'perfect' model answer. Use the questions you applied to your partner's response earlier, and decide whether aspects of this response could be improved.

Unseen poetry

What you have to do

In the exam for **Section C Unseen Poetry** you will have to write about two poems that you haven't previously read. To do this, you will use the skills you have developed during your GCSE course and from studying your chosen cluster of this book.

You will have copies of both poems in front of you and will have about 45 minutes to answer two questions:

- For Question 1, you will answer one question on one unseen poem.
- For Question 2, you will compare this poem with a second unseen poem.

How you will be assessed

Question 1 is worth 24 marks. You will be assessed on two Assessment Objectives (AOs):

AO1: Read, understand and respond to texts.

AO2: Analyse the language, form and structure used by a writer to create meaning and effects, using relevant subject terminology where appropriate.

Question 2 is worth 8 marks. You will be assessed on AO2 only.

What each question requires

Question 1 requires you to write about content (*what's* in the poem) and style (*how* the poem is written).

You will write about the poem's style in relation to its content, and analyse the choices the poet has made to express their ideas.

Question 2 requires you only to compare the **style** of the two poems – the choices the poets have made to express their ideas and how these affect the reader.

How these resources support you

This section will help you develop and improve approaches to the **Section C Unseen poetry** questions and provide strategies for focused writing in the timed conditions of the exam. You will:

- develop your approach in responding to and comparing unseen poems, using poem pairs 1 and 2
- improve your response, using poem pairs 3 and 4.

QUESTION 1: RESPONDING TO AN UNSEEN POEM

Step 1: Understand the question and the content of the poem

Take notice of the focus of the question. The practice question here is:

> In 'My Parents', how does the poet present the speaker's feelings about being bullied?

So it is clear that the poem will involve bullying.

1 Often the opening sentence acts like an anchor to help readers get a fix on key ideas and feelings that are developed later. The opening sentence of this poem is 'My parents kept me from children who were rough'. What does this suggest to you?

2 Now read the poem and the example of how one student began to make notes. Then write your own notes for each verse stating what you understand and any questions you have.

3 Share what you have understood so far with a partner. Then work together on any questions you still have about the poem.

My Parents

My parents kept me from children who were rough
Who threw words like stones and who wore torn clothes
Their thighs showed through rags. They ran in the street
And climbed cliffs and stripped by the country streams.

5   I feared more than tigers their muscles like iron
Their jerking hands and their knees tight on my arms
I feared the salt coarse pointing of those boys
Who copied my lisp behind me on the road.

They were lithe, they sprang out behind hedges
10 Like dogs to bark at my world. They threw mud
While I looked the other way, pretending to smile.
I longed to forgive them but they never smiled.

Stephen Spender

> First line sets up idea of poem about poet's parents protecting him from 'rough' kids.

> What the rough kids were like: torn clothes and rags, so poor? Sound wild, strong, running in streets, climbing cliffs, etc.

0 1   In 'My Parents', how does the poet present the speaker's feelings about being bullied?

[24 marks]

4 Focus on the question. What aspect of the poem do you have to write about? Make a spidergram showing what you know about the speaker being bullied and how the speaker feels. Add quotations to back up your ideas.

5 You should now have a good grasp of the poem's content. Check your understanding by discussing these questions with a partner:

a   What sort of people are the bullies?
b   Why do you think they bully?
c   What are the effects of the bullying on the victim? What tells you this?
d   Why do you think the poet wrote the poem?

Step 2: Explore the language of the poem

Next, focus on **how** the poet presents the speaker's feelings about being bullied. Focus on any places where the writer has used:

- effective adjectives, verbs or imagery (metaphors, simile, personification)
- effective sound techniques (rhythm, rhyme, alliteration, onomatopoeia and so on).

Remember every technique is used on purpose. When you notice a technique is being used, work out how it is helping the writer express the idea, attitude or feeling at this point in the poem.

1 Reread the poem, recognising five places where the writer has used techniques to present the speaker's feelings. For each one:

a   Name the technique, and explain how it is created. For example the simile 'Who threw words like stones' compares the way the words are thrown at him with stones being hurled at him.

b   Explain how using language in this way presents the speaker's feelings. For example this simile makes readers think about how much words hurt – stones can bruise or cut your skin, words can damage your feelings.

2 Find out what you have achieved by working with a partner to do these tasks.

a   Choose five words or phrases that describe the appearance and actions of the boys – look in particular at the poet's use of adjectives and similes.

b   Choose two details and write sentences to explain why they are effective. For example why do you think that the poet says 'Like dogs to bark at my world' rather than 'Like dogs to bark at me'?

c   The first line of the poem is a definite statement: 'My parents kept me from children who were rough'. Did they? How would you interpret 'kept me from'?

They were lithe, they sprang out behind hedges
Like dogs to bark at my world.

Step 3: Explore form and structure

The poet will have made careful choices about what form to write the poem in and what structure (organisation) to use to best express the ideas, attitudes and feelings.

Look out for these commonly used techniques (but remember, a technique is only worth writing about if you explain **how** the technique is used to express ideas, attitudes or feelings):

- patterns (for example organisation of verses, repeated rhythm, rhyme or words)
- accumulation – something being built up (for example a list)
- balance – the juxtaposition of one idea, person, place or idea against another
- contrasts – opposites of ideas, words, descriptions and so on
- developments – big changes in focus or ideas (for example from one time, character, place or situation to another). Sometimes poets use a gap (called a **caesura**) to emphasise the change has taken place.

1 Study the form and structure of this poem and decide which of the features listed above the writer has used. Then answer these questions:

a The poet often writes lines that are neatly balanced (words are juxtaposed) and create a contrast. For instance the last line of the poem might be annotated as follows:

I <u>longed to forgive</u> them but they <u>never smiled</u>.

> Doesn't bear grudge – desperate to be accepted

> Insensitive – result of tough background? Maintaining image?

Now annotate the underlined details in the first line in a similar way:

<u>My parents kept me from</u> <u>children who were rough</u>

Do you think that this is a good way to open the poem?

b Endings of poems are often important in emphasising key ideas. Poets often develop their ideas towards a powerful or significant climax. Do you think the last line is an effective ending? Explain your ideas.

c Look at which sections of the poem are presented in the third person ('they') and which in the first person ('I'). Can you see any pattern? Why might the poet have organised the poem in this way?

Step 4: Write about the poem

Now write a response to Question 1, using the text to back up your ideas:

0 1	In 'My Parents', how does the poet present the speaker's feelings about being bullied?

[24 marks]

> Remember: Question 1 is worth three times the marks for Question 2. You would have about 30 minutes to answer it.

181

QUESTION 2: COMPARING TWO UNSEEN POEMS

In Question 2 you will be asked to compare the first unseen poem with another one. Question 2 is worth 8 marks and you will have about 10 minutes to complete it in the exam. You will need to be quick, and you don't need to write everything you think about the poem, but what you do write needs to be relevant to the question.

You will not earn any marks for comparing the content of the two poems, only for comparing the way they are written – their style.

Step 1: Understand the question and the poem

Read the second unseen poem and question below.

Tich Miller

Tich Miller wore glasses
with elastoplast-pink frames
and had one foot three sizes larger than the other.

When they picked teams for outdoor games
5   she and I were always the last two
left standing by the wire-mesh fence.

We avoided one another's eyes,
stooping, perhaps, to re-tie a shoelace,
or affecting interest in the flight

10   of some fortunate bird, and pretended
not to hear the urgent conference:
'Have Tubby!' 'No, no, have Tich!'

Usually they chose me, the lesser dud,
and she lolloped, unselected,
15   to the back of the other team.

At eleven we went to different schools.
In time I learned to get my own back,
sneering at hockey-players who couldn't spell.

Tich died when she was twelve.

Wendy Cope

---

0 2   In both poems the speakers describe experiences of bullying. What are the similarities and/or differences between the ways the poets present those experiences?

[8 marks]

> Take notice of the focus of the question. Here, you know that the speakers in both poems describe experiences of bullying. You are asked what the similarities/differences are between the **ways** the poets present those experiences.

Step 2: Read the poem and note details

When you read the poem, choose at least four details of the way the speaker describes experiences of bullying. Compare them with details in the first poem.

Make sure you pick out some similarities and some differences. Some poems will have lots of similarities and some will have lots of differences, so the following bullet points are only a guide.

Think about:

- how language is used to describe people and place
- how language is used to describe feelings
- how the poems are organised – look at openings and endings in particular.

Search for:

- patterns of verbs, nouns, adjectives or adverbs
- images (similes, metaphors, personification)
- sound effects (for example onomatopoeia, rhyme and rhythm)
- form and structure.

1 Reread the poem. Then look at the following notes, which show the details one student has selected for this pair of poems.

If you are running out of time, your notes will still be marked for what you have identified, even if you have not turned them into full sentences.

Details on language – words and phrases: title/opening lines

Similarities: Both poets repeat heading in first line. Shows focus for presentation of experiences of bullying.

Differences:

Poem 1: Focus on bullies. Description of 'rough' children. Simile used to show action and strength of bullies: 'threw words like stones'.

Poem 2: Focus on victim. Words and phrases describe appearance of Tich. Give impression of her as vulnerable. Description of glasses links with ideas of hurt 'elastoplast-pink frames'.

Details on form and structure – last line/dialogue

Similarities: both poets use free verse. Both lead up to surprise in last line. Makes reader think more deeply about the poems.

Differences: Poem 2: Uses some dialogue. Reader experiences with Tich the impact of the words of the bullies.

she and I were always the last two left standing by the wire-mesh fence.

2 Now find four further details of similarities/differences to compare the ways the speakers describe the experience of bullying. Make notes and focus on what effect they have on the reader.

Work with a partner. Read the following paragraph in which a student compares the writers' methods in detail. Decide how she has:

a made it clear whether she has recognised a similarity or difference

b explained why each writer has used a particular method

c commented on how use of this method might affect the reader.

Both poets use the verb 'to pretend' in their poems and place the verb at the end of a line. The speaker in 'My Parents' says 'pretending to smile', which suggests the speaker is trying to appear friendly to the bullies, whereas the speaker in 'Tich Miller' says 'pretended / not to hear', hinting that they are trying to protect themselves by seeming not to notice what is going on. In both poems 'pretending' is used to suggest the victims are trying to cope with the bullying by looking as if they are not hurt by it. However, because the verb is at the end of the line it is emphasised, making the reader notice that it is only a pretence. The placement of the verb helps the reader realise what a serious impact the bullying actually has on the victim. It hurts.

Step 3: Write your comparison

Using your notes and the examples above, write a paragraph in answer to Question 2, in which you compare each of your chosen details:

0 2	In both poems the speakers describe experiences of bullying. What are the similarities and/or differences between the ways the poets present those experiences?

[8 marks]

Remember: In the exam, you only have about 10 minutes for all your work on Question 2. This question is worth only a third of the marks for Question 1.

Use your work in this unit and your learning from your cluster to respond to the following poems and questions.

Visiting Hour

The hospital smell
combs my nostrils
as they go bobbing along
green and yellow corridors.

5 What seems a corpse
is trundled into a lift and vanishes
heavenward.

I will not feel, I will not
feel, until
10 I have to.

Nurses walk lightly, swiftly,
here and up and down and there,
their slender waists miraculously
carrying their burden
15 of so much pain, so
many deaths, their eyes
still clear after
so many farewells.

Ward 7. She lies
20 in a white cave of forgetfulness.
A withered hand
trembles on its stalk. Eyes move
behind eyelids too heavy
to raise. Into an arm wasted
25 of colour a glass fang is fixed,
not guzzling but giving.
And between her and me
distance shrinks till there is none left
but the distance of pain that neither she nor I
30 can cross.

She smiles a little at this
black figure in her white cave
who clumsily rises
in the round swimming waves of a bell
35 and dizzily goes off, growing fainter,
not smaller, leaving behind only
books that will not be read
and fruitless fruits.

Norman MacCaig

0 1   In 'Visiting Hour' how does the poet
present the speaker's feelings about
visiting the sick woman?

[24 marks]

Tip

Remember, you may find it useful to take:

A four-step approach to Question 1 – focus, with notes on:

1 the question and the poem's content
2 the use and effect of language
3 the use and effect of structure and form
4 writing a focused response.

A three-step approach to Question 2 – focus, with notes, on comparing similarities and differences in:

1 the use and effect of language
2 the use and effect of structure and form
3 a focused comparison of style only.

Timing and focus
You do not need to use the timings of the exam in your work to develop skills in this unit. However, remember that in the exam:

• Question 1 on one unseen poem is worth 24 marks and you will have around 30 minutes to answer it. Spend around 5 minutes making notes.

• Question 2 is worth 8 marks and you will have around 10 minutes for all your work. You will need to work quickly to make brief notes and write your comparison.

185

Evans

Evans? Yes, many a time
I came down his bare flight
Of stairs into the gaunt kitchen
With its wood fire, where crickets sang
5 Accompaniment to the black kettle's
Whine, and so into the cold
Dark to smother in the thick tide
Of night that drifted about the walls
Of his stark farm on the hill ridge.

10 It was not the dark filling my eyes
And mouth appalled me; not even the drip
Of rain like blood from the one tree
Weather-tortured. It was the dark
Silting the veins of that sick man
15 I left stranded up on the vast
And lonely shore of his bleak bed.

R.S.Thomas

0 2 In both poems the speakers describe the experience of visiting a person who is old and sick. What are the similarities and/or differences between the ways the poets present these experiences?

[8 marks]

POINTS TO CONSIDER

Remember to support all interpretations with references to the text. You may want to think about the following:

'Visiting Hour'

- The **content** of the poem. For example the **sights/events** and **feelings** in each verse; the development of ideas to the end of the poem; why the poet wrote the poem.

- The **language** of the poem. For example the use and effect of sense impressions; vivid imagery; the words and phrases used to show feelings.

- The **structure and form** of the poem. For example how poem and verse openings involve the reader; how rhythm shows action; how the free verse form emphasises key words by placing them at the openings of lines.

'Evans'

- Remember, you are not assessed on content in Question 2. Notice the question states that in both poems the speakers describe the experience of visiting a person who is old and sick. Your focus in Question 2 is on **how** the poets' present the experiences effectively.

- The **language** of the poem. For example, use and effect of adjectives in describing setting and creating atmosphere and feeling; use of images to present experiences.

- The **structure and form** of the poem. For example, how poem and verse openings involve the reader; effective endings; use of verses to change emphasis; how the free verse form emphasises key words by placing them at the openings of lines.

Of his stark farm on the hill ridge.

This is not a test, but is designed to improve your skills and help you be prepared and confident for the exam. You will compare your responses with an example written by a student, identify its positive qualities, and think about possible ways of improving both it and your own responses. You will then apply your learning to improve your response to poem pair 4.

1 Start by reading and thinking about the poems and questions on the following two pages for about 10 minutes.

2 Write brief notes on the points you would make in answering Question 1. (Remember that in the exam you would have about 30 minutes to write your response.)

3 Make brief notes on the points you would make in answering Question 2. (Remember

that in the exam you would only have about 10 minutes to write your response.)

4 When you have done this, exchange your notes with a partner and answer the following questions:

a Have you both planned to make similar points?

b Has either of you made points the other hasn't?

c Have all points been made clearly? If not, check what your partner intended to say.

d Are there things you disagree about?

e Have the points been supported with references to the poems? If not, can you suggest which details might have been used to back up the points?

Sparrow

He's no artist.
His taste in clothes is more
dowdy than gaudy.
And his nest – that blackbird, writing
5   pretty scrolls on the air with the gold nib of
       his beak,
would call it a slum.

To stalk solitary on lawns,
to sing solitary in midnight trees,
to glide solitary over gray Atlantics –
10   not for him: he'd rather
a punch-up in a gutter.

He carries what learning he has
lightly – it is, in fact, based only
on the usefulness whose result
15   is survival. A proletarian bird.
No scholar.

But when winter soft-shoes in
and these other birds –
ballet dancers, musicians, architects –
20   die in the snow
and freeze to branches,
watch him happily flying
on the O-levels and A-levels
of the air.

Norman MacCaig

proletarian (15) – of the lowest class in society
O-levels (23) – exams (they were replaced by GCSEs)

0 1   In 'Sparrow', how does the poet present the speaker's attitudes towards and feelings about the bird?

[24 marks]

Terrorist

One morning I despaired of writing more,
    never any more,
when a swallow swooped in, around and out
    the open door
5   then in again and batlike to the window,
    against which
beating himself, a suicide in jail,
    he now and then collapsed into
his midnight iridescent combat suit,
10   beautiful white markings on the tail.

Inside his balaclava, all he knew
    was something light and airy he had
      come from
flattened into something hard and blue.
    Thank God for all those drafts I used to
15 scoop, shove or shovel him to the transom,
    open just enough to let him through.

Off he flew, writing his easy looped
    imaginary line.
No sign of his adventure left behind
20   but my surprise
and his – not fright, though he had
    frightened me, those two
bright high-tech bullets called his eyes.
    What they said was
25 'Fight and fight and fight. No compromise.'

Anne Stevenson

transom (15) – bar on a window

0 2   In both 'Sparrow' and 'Terrorist' the speakers describe attitudes towards and feelings about different birds. What are the main similarities and differences between the ways the poets present those attitudes and feelings?

[8 marks]

Ways to show your response skills

As you make notes, think about how you could cover the following points:

- **Focus:** start at least three paragraphs by referring to words in the question.
- **Language:** explain what other word would have fitted, but less well than the chosen word, so why it is a good choice by the writer.
- **Detail:** write one short paragraph about one small detail of the text.
- **Comparison:** when you've compared the poems and found a similarity, add something that shows a contrast (the 'Both … but …' technique).
- **Rereading:** show how your response to the poem changed from your first reading because of your deeper understanding from a later reading.

his midnight iridescent combat suit,
beautiful white markings on the tail.

EVALUATING RESPONSES

Note that the following responses are not model ('perfect') answers. They were written in exam conditions, and so under time pressure. **Remember that you cannot and do not have to make every possible point to do well in the exam.**

Example response to practice Question 1, on 'Sparrow'

The poet presents a negative view of the bird at the beginning ✔ when he states 'His taste in clothes is more/dowdy than gaudy' which means that the bird – which can be interpreted to mean a human ✔ – is boring rather than flamboyant as he does not care for the opinion of others. Compared to other birds, the sparrow is boring and not as interesting.

> ✔ Concise, direct opening – relevant comment about poet's intentions

> ✔ Understands implied symbolism

The poet also presents the bird as poor and unsanitary when he presents a blackbird (which can be perceived to mean a rich and intelligent person) in a positive way ✔ and writes 'pretty scrolls on the air with the gold nib of his beak', stating that the sparrow lives in a 'slum' and is a 'proletarian bird' – of the lowest class in society – which shows that the sparrow is a person who is a social reject or society's outcast. ✔ This is also shown with the repetition of the adjective 'solitary', ✔ which shows him to be alone in his endeavours, but this is modified ✔ when the poet says 'he'd rather / a punch-up in a gutter' which shows him to be argumentative and looking for a fight. This helps convey the speaker's negative perception of the sparrow and helps the reader to share that point of view. ✔

> ✔ Hints at use of contrast without commenting

> ✔ Develops understanding of symbolism

> ✔ Effective comment on poet's technique

> ✔ Understanding of structure – how poet deliberately changes reader's response

> ✔ Makes clear how poet intends reader to respond

In the third verse, it is stressed that the sparrow is 'no scholar', implying that he is not as well educated as the other birds. However, the poet also states in the fourth verse that whilst the other, more attractive birds 'die in the snow', the sparrow is 'happily flying / on the O-levels and A-levels / of the air', proving that whilst his intelligence and attractiveness are lacking, his survival skills are above those of the other birds. ✔

> ✔ Uses selected details to show understanding of poem's final 'message'

Example response to practice Question 2, on 'Terrorist'

Both of the poets have chosen to write about birds as they are normally seen to be majestic. However, both of the two poems do not show the birds to be elegant. 'Sparrow' presents the bird as boring, 'dowdy', uneducated, 'no scholar' and dangerous – 'he'd rather / a punch up in a gutter'. Moreover, 'Terrorist' also presents the bird as dangerous: 'he had / frightened me'. ✔ This causes the reader to experience a conflict between stereotypes and what is presented in the poem.

However, the two poems are also different in many senses. 'Sparrow' is showing the bird as a metaphor for a person, whilst 'Terrorist' focuses on the effect that a literal bird has on the poet but uses the extended metaphor of the terrorist to show that the bird seems threatening. ✔

✔ Uses language details to illustrate how birds are presented

✔ Comments effectively on purposes/effects of metaphor by two poets

Commentary on the responses

1 Now read the expert commentary on the responses. Then assess your own responses, or those of another student, against the examples and comments above, and the points made below.

2 Use these points to recognise your strengths and the areas that you need to improve when you tackle poem pair 4.

Question 1: Strong features of the student's answer:

- the concise, well-organised and direct approach
- the focus on 'the poet' to comment on the writer's intentions
- the consistent use of concise and relevant quotations to support interpretations
- the relevant use of terminology.

There are no 'right' answers. Other students might have made different and equally relevant points, such as:

- The poem is quite 'blunt' and matter-of fact in tone – as if to reflect the 'no-nonsense' nature of the sparrow's character.
- Short sentences or isolated phrases are often used to emphasise details and help to create this 'bluntness' – often effective as the closing lines of verses.
- By contrast, the description of the blackbird is longer and uses more elaborate descriptive language.
- The poem's structure is based on contrast, and the last verse shows the positive qualities of the sparrow, the change in the direction of the poem being signalled by the opening word 'But'.
- It is significant that the poet ends with the word 'air', which emphasises the bird's freedom.

Question 2: The answer shows the positive qualities identified in Question 1, and meets the requirements of the question by consciously comparing the styles of the two poems.

It is difficult to write much in the time available for this second answer, but other possible points might have been:

- In 'Sparrow', the poet generalises about the features of the bird to communicate his ideas, whereas in 'Terrorist' the poet uses a personal experience to explore the nature of the bird and the speaker's attitudes towards it; the latter speaker is presented as more emotionally involved with the bird than the former.
- Although in 'Terrorist' the speaker partly admires the bird, both poets try to change the reader's perceptions – a swallow is generally considered graceful but is seen here as partly threatening; a sparrow is thought of as ordinary, but is seen here as having important skills.
- Both poems build up to a forceful climax, a presentation of the key idea or 'message'.
- In 'Sparrow', the poet uses the free-verse form flexibly, often emphasising key words at the openings of lines, for example 'is survival'; 'Terrorist' has a regular pattern of alternating long and short lines – an attempt to suggest the general flight pattern of swallows, and the panic experienced by this one in particular?

Save the Children
Djibouti 1961… Biafra 1971… Eritrea 1981…

And suddenly the crowd flowed,
Gathering in a corner of the square
As though the wind that sifted
The dunes into the wells had blown them there.
5　They milled and struggled where the sand had drifted,
Their kaftans covering
The boxes like the vultures' wings
That canopy a carcase while their beaks
Rummage and tussle at the bloody fat.
10　Latecomers on the fringes could not see
What sort of alms they burrowed at.
A sinewy teenager jumped back out,
His shirt-front angular with loot,
Raced for the camel market through a file
15　Of straight-backed women bearing
Their petrol tins of water on their heads
Like priceless antique loads.

Beside the heaving townsfolk, past all caring,
Leaning against the polished hardwood door
20　Of the *Chambre de Commerce* whose flagstaff
Rose white and naked minus its *tricolor*,
A boy of twelve was standing, staring
From swollen eyes like avocado stones
Set in his peeling melon-head.
25　His fingers, jointed like a lemur's,
Bunched loosely round a tin
Of John West choice sardines.
His legs were bamboo-thin,
His knees were gourds, his blackness hung in shreds
30　From scalp and chest and thighs.
I could not bear to look at him. He could
Not look at all. His fused-out eyes
Were pointed far beyond
To where his life ran out in sand.

David Craig

kaftans (7) – loose-fitting robes
Chambre de Commerce (21) – trading centre
tricolor (22) – the French flag (three-coloured)
lemur (26) – an animal similar to a monkey
gourds (30) – fruits similar to melons and pumpkins

0 1　In 'Save the Children', how does the poet present the situation
　(the delivery of food aid in a developing country) and the
　speaker's feelings about it?

[24 marks]

Complete this assignment
on Cambridge Elevate

1 Now read and respond to the questions for poem pair 4.

2 When you have completed your responses, swap with a partner and give feedback in light of your work on poem pair 3. Where is your answer strong? Where might you focus your efforts to improve?

Blessing

The skin cracks like a pod.
There never is enough water.

Imagine the drip of it,
the small splash, echo
5   in a tin mug,
the voice of a kindly god.

Sometimes, the sudden rush
of fortune. The municipal pipe bursts,
silver crashes to the ground
10 and the flow has found
a roar of tongues. From the huts,
a congregation: every man woman
child for streets around
butts in, with pots,
15 brass, copper, aluminium,
plastic buckets,
frantic hands,

and naked children
screaming in the liquid sun,
20 their highlights polished to perfection,
flashing light,
as the blessing sings
over their small bones.

Imtiaz Dharker

---

0 2   Both poems describe events in developing countries.
What are the similarities and/or differences between
the ways the poets present these experiences?

[8 marks]

Complete this assignment on
Cambridge Elevate

as the blessing sings
over their small bones.

Preparing for your exam

Poetry is assessed in your GCSE English Literature Paper 2 examination, **Modern texts and poetry**. The paper lasts for 2 hours and 15 minutes so you have around 45 minutes for each section. It is worth 60% of your GCSE in English Literature.

Paper 2 has three sections:
In **Section A Modern texts**, you answer **one** essay question from a choice of two on your studied modern prose or drama text.

In **Section B Poetry**, you answer **one** question on comparing poems from your chosen cluster of the anthology, 'Love and relationships' or 'Power and conflict'. There are 30 marks for this question.

In **Section C Unseen poetry**, you first write about a poem that you have not seen before (24 marks) and then compare this poem with a second unseen poem (8 marks).

How to approach Section B Poetry

You will need to answer **one** question on comparing poems from your chosen cluster of the anthology. You have roughly 45 minutes for this question, which is worth 30 marks.

- The question will select one poem from your chosen cluster of the anthology, and this poem will be printed on the question paper.
- You will choose another poem from your chosen cluster to compare it with, and you will be working from memory with that poem. You will not have the anthology with you in the exam.

The Assessment Objective skills

For Section B, your answers will be assessed against three Assessment Objectives (AOs). Notice the marks for each AO and take account of this as you manage your time and focus your response.

AO1: Read, understand and respond to texts. You should be able to:
- maintain a critical style and develop an informed personal response
- use textual references, including quotations, to support and illustrate interpretations. (12 marks)

AO2: Analyse the language, form and structure used by a writer to create meanings and effects, using relevant subject terminology where appropriate. (12 marks)

AO3: Show understanding of the relationships between texts and the context in which they were written. (6 marks)

What to do in the exam

- Read the question carefully. Make sure you understand its focus and select a poem to compare that relates to the question focus and will give you plenty to say.
- Make notes before you answer the question, so you are prepared.
- Structure your answer and make a focused comparison that shows your skills.

Cluster 1: Love and relationships

You can use this example question to help you prepare and practise your skills for the exam. The following pages will help you to assess your skills so that you know what you do well and can focus on areas to improve.

Read the practice question and annotations below, and use the skills you have developed to respond to the question.

Mother, any distance

Mother, any distance greater than a single span
requires a second pair of hands.
You come to help me measure windows, pelmets, doors,
the acres of the walls, the prairies of the floors.

5   You at the zero-end, me with the spool of tape, recording
length, reporting metres, centimetres back to base, then leaving
up the stairs, the line still feeding out, unreeling
years between us. Anchor. Kite.

I space-walk through the empty bedrooms, climb
10   the ladder to the loft, to breaking point, where something has to give;
two floors below your fingertips still pinch
the last one-hundredth of an inch … I reach
towards a hatch that opens on an endless sky
to fall or fly.

Simon Armitage

Compare how poets present attitudes to family relationships in 'Mother, any distance' and in **one** other poem from 'Love and relationships'.

[30 marks]

> You need to compare two poems (AO1).

> Focus on the writer, to think about how the poet presents attitudes (AO2).

> This directs you to the 'named' poem, printed on the paper.

> This asks you to think about contexts and gives you the subject that you need to stick to in your response (AO3).

> You have a free choice about which poem to choose from your cluster.

 Complete this assignment on Cambridge Elevate

ASSESS YOUR SKILLS

The following extracts are from sample responses to the practice question. They provide examples of skills at different levels when writing for GCSE English Literature.

Here, the poem chosen to compare with 'Mother, any distance' is Seamus Heaney's 'Follower'. There is no 'right' poem to compare. You need to be able to meet the focus of the question and support your comparison with references from the text.

Compare the extracts with your own answer to the question. As you read the extracts, think about how far each example – and your own answer – is successful in:

- supporting comments with details from the text
- making use of details from the text to build interpretation
- linking detail with the poet's craft in writing poetry and the poet's purpose in conveying ideas or attitudes.

Student A

This is taken from early in Student A's response:

Simon Armitage presents the relationship between a mother and a son in this poem. I am going to compare his poem with Seamus Heaney's poem 'Follower', which is also about a parent-child relationship, but about the relationship between a son and a father.

Armitage presents the relationship at the moment the son leaves home to live on his own, which is a big move in life. He uses words that make his new house seem like a huge area with words like 'acres' and 'prairies' to give you the idea he's setting off on an adventure. It's an adventure because he's getting away from the 'anchor' who is his mother, and he doesn't know if he can fly on his own or fall to earth. He'd like to be like a kite, that still has strings to bring it back.

Seamus Heaney also presents a change in the relationship, but his change is one caused by time and age. He uses words that show a contrast between the father as a young man, watched by Heaney as a boy, when his father was strong and an expert at ploughing. Heaney makes the father seem in control by describing his control of the plough and the horses, and himself as a boy clumsy and weak ('I stumbled', 'Fell sometimes'). But now that his father is old, it is the father who 'keeps stumbling' as if the roles are reversed.

This is taken from further on in Student A's response:

In both of these poems the writers show the relationship between a child and a parent, but in 'Follower' the relationship changes, as the child grows up and the father grows older. In 'Mother, any distance', the poem is focused on the moment the son leaves home, and you get more of a sense of the parent's feelings as well as the son's feelings.

Student A shows the following skills in these parts of the response:

- focus on the task
- effective use of details from the text to support comments on the writers' ideas
- explanation of the writers' use of language for purpose and effect
- understanding of feelings and relationships.

Student B

This is taken from early in Student B's response:

'Mother, any distance' is a poem that explores the ambivalence of a young man leaving home to set up on his own. His mother is helping him to move but also feels ambivalent, symbolically shown by her clinging on to 'pinching' the end of the measuring tape that records the increasing distance between them.

The character in the poem (possibly Armitage himself) is excited at exploring the 'acres' and 'prairies' of his new flat as an adventure in a wide new unknown territory, but as he reaches the top floor, he realises that he has been used to his mother as his point of stability and safety ('anchor') allowing him to soar away like a 'kite', but still on string. The excitement turns to fear as he realises that he is finally moving away from her, and he will have to do without the 'strings' and take a risk of 'flying' on his own, or 'falling'. That's what makes his new independence a double-edged thing.

'Follower' is also a poem that explores ambivalence in a child-parent relationship. Heaney's angle on this is different from Armitage's because he recalls the past affection and admiration he had as a child for his father's skill in 'clicking' the horses, 'mapping' the ground and adjusting the 'wing' of the plough. As a child, he was the one who 'stumbled' and was a nuisance, but now his father and he have swapped roles, where the father is now the one who 'keeps stumbling' and is a nuisance.

This is taken from further on in Student B's response:

I think both of these writers have explored two sides of a relationship, Armitage looking at the contrast between security and independence at the point where he leaves home, and Heaney looking at the contrast between past expertise and present physical decay at the point where he is now the fully functioning adult.

Student B shows the following skills in these parts of the response:

- strong focus on the task
- convincing use of details from the text to support interpretation of the writers' ideas
- analysis of language choices for purpose and effect
- exploration of feelings and relationships.

Use what you have learned from this section to focus on skills to improve for your exam.

Cluster 2: Power and conflict

You can use this example question to help you prepare and practise your skills for the exam. The following pages will help you to assess your skills so that you know what you do well and can focus on areas to improve.

Read the practice question and annotations below, and use the skills you have developed to respond to the question.

Complete this assignment on Cambridge Elevate

Extract from The Prelude

One summer evening (led by her) I found
A little boat tied to a willow tree
Within a rocky cove, its usual home.
Straight I unloosed her chain, and stepping in
5   Pushed from the shore. It was an act of stealth
And troubled pleasure, nor without the voice
Of mountain-echoes did my boat move on;
Leaving behind her still, on either side,
Small circles glittering idly in the moon,
10 Until they melted all into one track
Of sparkling light. But now, like one who rows,
Proud of his skill, to reach a chosen point
With an unswerving line, I fixed my view
Upon the summit of a craggy ridge,
15 The horizon's utmost boundary; far above
Was nothing but the stars and the grey sky.
She was an elfin pinnace; lustily
I dipped my oars into the silent lake,
And, as I rose upon the stroke, my boat
20 Went heaving through the water like a swan;
When, from behind that craggy steep till then
The horizon's bound, a huge peak, black and huge,
As if with voluntary power instinct,

25 Upreared its head. I struck and struck again,
And growing still in stature the grim shape
Towered up between me and the stars, and still,
For so it seemed, with purpose of its own
And measured motion like a living thing,
30 Strode after me. With trembling oars I turned,
And through the silent water stole my way
Back to the covert of the willow tree;
There in her mooring-place I left my bark, –
And through the meadows homeward went, in grave
35 And serious mood; but after I had seen
That spectacle, for many days, my brain
Worked with a dim and undetermined sense
Of unknown modes of being; o'er my thoughts
There hung a darkness, call it solitude
40 Or blank desertion. No familiar shapes
Remained, no pleasant images of trees,
Of sea or sky, no colours of green fields;
But huge and mighty forms, that do not live
Like living men, moved slowly through the mind
By day, and were a trouble to my dreams.

William Wordsworth

Compare the ways poets present ideas about the power of nature in 'The Prelude' extract and in **one** other poem from 'Power and conflict'.

[30 marks]

You need to compare two poems (AO1).

Focus on the writer, to think about ways the poet presents ideas (AO2).

This asks you to think about contexts and gives you the subject that you need to stick to in your response (AO3).

This directs you to the 'named' poem, printed on the paper.

You have a free choice about which poem to choose from your cluster.

ASSESS YOUR SKILLS

The following extracts are from sample responses to the practice question. They provide examples of skills at different levels when writing for GCSE English Literature.

Here, the poem chosen to compare with 'The Prelude' extract is 'Storm on the Island' by Seamus Heaney. There is no 'right' poem to compare. You need to be able to meet the focus of the question and support your comparison with references from the text.

Compare the extracts with your own answer to the question. As you read the extracts, think about how far each example – and your own answer – is successful in:

- supporting comments with details from the text
- making use of details from the text to build interpretation
- linking detail with the poet's craft in writing poetry and the poet's purpose in conveying ideas or attitudes.

Student A

This is taken from early in Student A's response:

Wordsworth presents the power of nature in this poem as something frightening but with a good side to it. Wordsworth was excited by taking the boat, because he calls it an 'elfin pinnace', which means a fairy or a magic boat. He shows his enthusiasm for rowing with the word 'lustily' when he dipped the oars. This is because he wants to convey the child's excitement and pleasure in the rowing and the beauty of the place.

Wordsworth makes the scene beautiful and calm by describing the ripples in the moonlight and the water as 'small circles glittering idly in the moon'. Then he contrasts this with the frightening appearance of the mountains, which are 'craggy', 'black and huge', making him feel 'serious'. This disturbing sense carries on later when he is at home, when his imagination makes him think of 'huge and mighty forms' that were 'a trouble to my dreams'. He personifies the mountain by making it seem out to get him.

This is taken from further on in Student A's response:

Heaney also uses personification of natural forces when he writes about the natural surroundings being frightening because of the force of the wind 'pummelling' and like an enemy, but the good that comes out of this power of nature is that the people who survive it are made stronger.

Both of these poems show nature as part of the culture that makes people the way they are. In 'Storm on the Island' the people have to learn to live without natural shelter, so they have to make their own. In 'The Prelude', Wordsworth is showing how a small boy can be influenced by his environment. In both cases it's a bit like nature is a parent or teacher.

Student A shows the following skills in these parts of the response:

- focus on the task
- effective use of details from the text to support comment on the writers' ideas
- explanation of the writers' use of language for purpose and effect
- understanding of the writers' ideas.

Student B

This is taken from early in Student B's response:

The extract from Wordsworth's poem 'The Prelude' explores the power of nature by showing its effect on a small boy taking someone else's boat for a row on the lake, which he describes as a 'troubled pleasure' which suggests he had a conscience about taking the boat. In the child's imagination, a mountain coming into view 'upreared its head' personifying it as a living monster coming to punish him for taking the boat. Wordsworth uses this scenario to represent the way that humans may learn something about 'unknown modes of being', such as morality, from the natural environment, but the learning may not be comfortable, as it was 'a trouble to my dreams'.

'Storm on the Island' is also a poem that explores the effect of nature, on people who live on an island. Heaney doesn't show nature to be a moral influence, though. He shows it to be a harsh environment 'wizened earth' personified with wind that 'pummels', which makes the people who live there tough and capable of putting up with hardship: 'We are prepared'. It is as though the harsh environment develops their character, making them able to survive rather than rely on comforts and protections like 'stacks or stooks'. In that way, nature may be frightening in its power but in both poems the writers show that that frightening power can have some positive results.

This is taken from further on in Student B's response:

I think both of these writers have explored the positive and the negative aspects of nature's power. Wordsworth brought out the power of the landscape to frighten a boy and make him wonder about dark and monstrous shapes in his imagination or real life. This is a common theme in Romantic poetry, which valued the imagination more than the reason, and the country more than the city. It also suggested that morality may develop from nature rather than religion or law. Heaney brought out the power of the weather to destroy, but also the power people got from resisting it and surviving.

Student B shows the following skills in these parts of the response:

- strong focus on the task
- convincing use of details from the text to support interpretation of the writers' ideas
- analysis of language choices for purpose and effect
- convincing exploration of ideas within and around the poem.

Use what you have learned from this section to focus on skills to improve for your exam.

Section C Unseen poetry

How to approach Section C Unseen Poetry

In **Section C Unseen poetry**, you first write about a poem that you have not seen before (24 marks) and then compare this poem with a second unseen poem (8 marks).

Notice the marks for each question and take account of this as you manage your time and focus your response. You have roughly 45 minutes for this section.

The Assessment Objective skills

Paper 2 has three sections:

For the first part of the question on one poem, your answers will be assessed against two Assessment Objectives (AOs) and each is worth 12 marks:

AO1: Read, understand and respond to texts. You should be able to:

* maintain a critical style and develop an informed personal response
* use textual references, including quotations, to support and illustrate interpretations.

AO2: Analyse the language, form and structure used by a writer to create meanings and effects, using relevant subject terminology where appropriate.

For the second part of the question, comparing the poem with a second unseen poem, your answer will be assessed only against AO2, and is worth 8 marks.

What to do in the exam

* Read the questions carefully. Make sure you understand the focus that is given with each question.
* For your response to a single unseen poem, it is probably useful to spend a few minutes making brief notes on the poem before you start to write. You might want to spend about 30 minutes on this question.
* For your comparison of the poem with a second unseen poem, the question outlines the focus for comparison. You will have a shorter amount of time to note any details before starting to write.
* Structure your responses so that you show your skills using focused writing on the poem on its own, and with the poem to compare.

There is guidance on the above and ways of approaching unseen poems in the **Unseen poetry** section of this book. You will also find guidance on planning and writing a comparative response in **Exploring and comparing poetry**.

You can use these example questions to help you prepare and practise your skills for the exam. Read the questions and annotations, and use the skills you have developed to respond to each question. Then use the following pages to help you to assess your skills so that you know what you do well and can focus on areas to improve.

They Did Not Expect This

They did not expect this. Being neither wise nor brave
And wearing only the beauty of youth's season
They took the first turning quite unquestioningly
And walked quickly without looking back even once.

5   It was of course the wrong turning. First they were nagged
By a small wind that tugged at their clothing like a dog;
Then the rain began and there was no shelter anywhere,
Only the street and the rows of houses stern as soldiers.

Though the blood chilled, the endearing word burnt the tongue.
10   There were no parks or gardens or public houses:
Midnight settled and the rain paused leaving the city
Enormous and still like a great sleeping seal.

At last they found accommodation in a cold
Furnished room where they quickly learnt to believe in ghosts;
15   They had their hope stuffed and put on the mantelpiece
But found, after a while, that they did not notice it.

While she spends many hours looking in the bottoms of teacups
He reads much about association football
And waits for the marvellous envelope to fall:
20   Their eyes are strangers and they rarely speak.
They did not expect this.

Vernon Scannell

Focus on the single poem.

In 'They Did Not Expect This', how does the poet present the relationship of the two people?

Focus on the writer, to think about how the poet presents the relationship of the two people.

[24 marks]

This part of the question is assessed against AO1 and AO2, for 12 marks each.

 Complete this assignment on Cambridge Elevate

The Pond

The heart had already gone out of our house
the summer you dug the pond. Day after
day, driving the old spade into clay,
bare-backed, your white limbs twitching
5   on the parched lawn, carving a womb.

I fought with dough in the dead kitchen:
brown bread for you, white for me.
We never ate together. You'd break pieces
from your loaf before it cooled – your usual
10   hurry to be somewhere else.

I wished the words the priest had made me say
unspoken, as I pressed the pill marked Thursday
from the packet. Standing beside the bed
I could not look out at the unfilled pond.

15   Empty of you, I pace through the rooms
on the upper floors. So many rooms
without a nursery air.

Kathryn Daszkiewicz

In both 'They Did Not Expect This' and 'The Pond', the speakers <u>describe love</u> <u>relationships</u>. <u>What are the similarities and/or differences</u> between the <u>ways the</u> <u>poets present</u> these relationships?

[8 marks]

This is the focus for comparison.

You can compare similarities and/ or differences.

This part of the question is assessed against AO2 only, for 8 marks.

Focus on each writer, to think about how the poet presents these relationships.

Answer **both** questions in this section.

Complete this assignment on Cambridge Elevate

ASSESS YOUR SKILLS

The following extracts are from sample responses to the practice questions. They provide examples of skills at different levels when writing for GCSE English Literature.

Compare the extracts with your own answer to the questions. As you read the extracts, think about how far each example – and your answer – is successful in:

* supporting comments with details from the text
* making use of details to build interpretation
* linking detail with the poet's craft in writing poetry and the poet's purpose in conveying ideas or attitudes.

> In 'They Did Not Expect This', how does the poet present the relationship of the two people?
>
> **[24 marks]**

Student A

The poet presents the relationship between the two people as a sad one because they have spent their life together but end up not talking to each other. He describes their togetherness as like a journey when you take the wrong path and end up somewhere you wouldn't want to go. This is a metaphor.

What makes Scannell's presentation of the couple sad is that they have given up their shared hope, 'hope stuffed and put on the mantelpiece', but they 'did not notice it'. Instead they live with their own hopes, like his dream of a winning 'envelope' from the football pools and her dreams of something in the future from reading the tea leaves (like a fortune teller).

He presents the relationship after a lifetime together as sad because now they don't look at each other ('Their eyes are strangers'). The last line is very sad because 'They did not expect this' means they thought that life would be better, but it's too late now because they took the wrong path when they were younger.

Student A shows the following skills in this extract from the response:
- focus on the task
- effective use of details from the text
- explanation of the writer's use of language for purpose and effect
- explanation of ideas.

Student B

The poet presents the relationship between the two people by using the extended metaphor of a journey. It is a journey that involved a wrong choice of direction – a 'wrong turning'. As co-travellers, the couple started on their journey together (the journey is marriage) without thinking too much about where their journey may lead them. They started out 'unquestioningly' and the poet suggests that this was because they were naïve, 'wearing only the beauty of youth's season'.

At the end of the poem, he shows how their journey ended, with the 'cold furnished room' symbolically representing a marriage without warmth, each wrapped up in their separate interests and their separate dreams, and remembering 'ghosts' from the past. She looks for something better forecast in the tea leaves, and he looks for something better in his football pools. The sad conclusion is that, despite travelling life's path together (metaphorically), they have ended up as strangers. The last line makes you realise that none of us knows when we are young how we will end up when we are old. It's not a cheerful thought, and Scannell seems to present us with a horrible warning about what follows youthful decisions based on the 'endearing word' which probably means 'Love'.

Student B shows the following skills in this extract from the response:
- strong focus on the task
- exploration of implications of details from the text
- exploration and analysis of the writer's use of language for purpose and effect
- exploration of the wider significance of ideas in the poem.

In both 'They Did Not Expect This' and 'The Pond', the speakers describe love relationships. What are the similarities and/or differences between the ways the poets present these relationships?

[8 marks]

Remember that in this question your answer and the similarities and/or differences you compare should be about AO2 **only** – that is, the methods the poet uses, with aspects of language, form and structure.

Student A

This writer also uses an extended metaphor to show how the relationship between two people has turned bad. The poet makes the pond seem like the husband's main interest, like the football in the first poem, but he links it to her main interest, which is to have a child. He does this by calling the pond 'a womb', and by referring to her womb as an 'unfilled pond'. Like the poet in the first poem, this one makes the sad relationship seem like a mistake by using images of past promise, like the words the priest made her say which she wishes were 'unspoken'.

Student A shows the following skills in this extract from the response:
* focus on the task (AO2)
* explanation of some of the writer's methods
* explanation of the effects of the writer's language choices.

Student B

The poet uses a metaphor to show the emptiness of the couple's marriage, like the 'stuffed' hope in the first poem. This poem uses the metaphor of the pond the husband is making. Like the husband's dream of a 'marvellous envelope' this represents the private activity in their shared life. The writer links the hollow pond with the woman's dreams by describing it as a 'womb'. This is important because she obviously wants a child, but that dream won't happen because of her birth control. Like the first poem, the poet uses an extended metaphor by describing her womb as an 'unfilled pond'. The poet emphasises the sadness of the couple's life the same way as the first poet, by images of separation – 'brown bread for you, white for me'. This makes the reader question whether small differences in taste may be a sign of differences in personality that can separate people. She regrets her past choices, wishing her marriage vows 'unspoken', which may make readers wonder about their own choices and where they end up.

Student B shows the following skills in this extract from the response:
* strong focus on the task (AO2)
* analysis of some of the writer's methods
* exploration of the effects of the writer's language choices.

Use what you have learned from this section to focus on skills to improve for your exam.

Glossary

alliteration the repetition of a letter or sound at the beginning of words (for example 'heartful of headlines' in 'Letters from Yorkshire' [see Cluster 1 Unit 8])

annotate write notes on a text to highlight details

assonance the repetition of a vowel sound for emphasis (for example 'six' and 'prick' in 'War Photographer' [see Cluster 2 Unit 11])

atmosphere the feelings created by a poet's description of a *setting*

blank verse poetry without rhyme but where the lines are always of the same number of syllables; it is usually written in *iambic pentameter*

chronological relating to the order in which things happen

cliché a very overused or unoriginal phrase

contemporary of our time; a contemporary poet is someone who is alive or who has died relatively recently

context the social, cultural and historical background of a text

contrast placing words, lines, verses and so on together to emphasise their differences (for example 'I was a nuisance, tripping, falling, / ... But today / It is my father who keeps stumbling / Behind me' from 'Follower' [see Cluster 1 Unit 10])

couplet a unit of two lines of poetry

dialect a form of a language used in a specific region or by a particular social group (see, for example, 'The Farmer's Bride' [Cluster 1 Unit 6])

dialogue a conversation between two or more people

diction a poet's choice of words such as verbs, adjectives and so on (for example the use of a pattern of adjectives in 'Evans' to suggest bareness and bleakness [see Unseen poetry, poem pair 2])

dramatic monologue a poem that takes the form of a speech by a fictional character (for example 'My Last Duchess' [see Cluster 2 Unit 4])

enjambement the overlapping of a sentence onto the following line, usually to emphasise a word or phrase at the start of a line (for example 'they sprang out behind hedges / Like dogs' in 'My Parents' [see Unseen poetry, poem pair 1])

extended metaphor a *metaphor* that is developed throughout a poem (for example the metaphor of thoughts as encircling vines in 'I think of thee!' [see Cluster 1 Unit 4])

first-person narrative an account of events written from a personal point of view (so using 'I' or 'we' rather than 'he/she' or 'they')

form the way a poem is set out

free verse poetry that does not have a regular pattern of rhyme

half-rhyme partial rhyme, which occurs when similar sounds are repeated at the ends of lines (for example 'sock' and 'pluck' on alternate lines in 'Follower' [see Cluster 1 Unit 10])

iambic pentameter the rhythm created by a line of ten syllables with five stressed syllables (for example 'I **think** of **thee**!—my **thoughts** do **twine** and **bud**' in 'I think of thee!' [see Cluster 1 Unit 4])

image a picture created with words, usually used to describe an imaginative comparison such as a *simile* or *metaphor*

implicit suggested but not directly stated

infer work out the meaning of something that is suggested – similar to *interpret*

interpret work out the meaning or significance of a section or detail in a text, such as an *image*

irony the use of words to imply the opposite of, or something different from, what is said (for example 'This wizened earth has never troubled us / With hay' in 'Storm on the Island' [see Cluster 2 Unit 7])

justify back up a point with evidence (from a text)

metaphor an *image* or imaginative comparison in which one thing is said to be another (for example 'Space is a salvo' in 'Storm on the Island' [see Cluster 2 Unit 7])

monologue a long speech spoken by a single character, usually revealing inner feelings

narrative an account of events or a story, told by a narrator (for example 'The Farmer's Bride' [see Cluster 1 Unit 6])

onomatopoeia the use of a word that sounds like its meaning (for example 'the black kettle's / Whine' in 'Evans' [see Unseen poetry, poem pair 2])

oxymoron a phrase containing an apparent contradiction (for example 'fruitless fruits' in 'Visiting Hour' [see Unseen poetry, poem pair 2])

pace the speed at which a poem flows (for example the fast pace created by *alliteration* in 'Sudden successive flights of bullets streak the silence' in 'Exposure' [see Cluster 2 Unit 6])

persona the 'speaker' in a poem who is a created 'character' rather than the poet him or herself

personification the *poetic device* of giving human qualities to an object (for example 'Dawn massing in the east her melancholy army' in 'Exposure' [see Cluster 2 Unit 6])

perspective an attitude towards something, a point of view

poetic device a technique used by a poet, for example use of *similes* or repetition

prose any piece of writing that is not in *verse* form

pun a 'play on words'; the use of a word or phrase with a double meaning (for example 'salient' in 'Exposure' [see Cluster 2 Unit 6])

refrain a recurring phrase or set of lines (for example the repetition of 'Cannon to right of them, / Cannon to left of them,' in 'The Charge of the Light Brigade' [see Cluster 2 Unit 5])

rhyme scheme the pattern of a poem's rhyme, often identified by letters such as ABAB

rhythm the pattern of sounds or 'movement' in a poem (for example the use of rhyme in 'The Charge of the Light Brigade' [see Cluster 2 Unit 5] creates a fast, regular *pace*)

setting the description of the place in which a poem is set

simile an imaginative comparison that uses 'like' or 'as' (for example 'His shoulders globed like a full sail strung' in 'Follower' [see Cluster 1 Unit 10])

sonnet a poem of 14 lines with a distinctive *rhyme scheme* (for example 'I think of thee!' [see Cluster 1 Unit 4])

standard English the variety of English used in public communication (not *dialect* or slang)

stanza a group of lines forming a unit in a poem, also known as a *verse*

structure the way a poem is organised (for example the separation of the final line for emphasis in 'Tich Miller' [see Unseen poetry, poem pair 1])

symbol something that is used to represent something else (for example the swallow in 'Terrorist' [see Unseen poetry, poem pair 3])

sympathetic background a *setting* that matches the situation and enhances the mood of characters (for example the dismal, wintry setting of 'Neutral Tones' [see Cluster 1 Unit 5])

syntax sentence structure

tone feelings or ideas suggested by words (for example the sense of excitement created in 'Blessing' [see Unseen poetry, poem pair 4])

verse (mass noun) another word for poetry; (noun) a group of lines forming a unit in a poem, also known as a *stanza*

viewpoint the position from which the poet or a character sees things

volta a 'turning point' in a *sonnet*, usually occurring after the eighth line and often signified by words such as 'But' or 'And yet' (for example 'And on the pedestal these words appear:' in 'Ozymandias' [see Cluster 2 Unit 1])

Produced for Cambridge University Press by White-Thomson Publishing

+44 (0)843 208 7460

www.wtpub.co.uk

Project editor: Rachel Minay
Designer: Kim Williams, 320 Media
Picture research: Izzi Howell